Contents

Contents

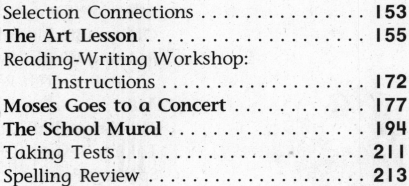

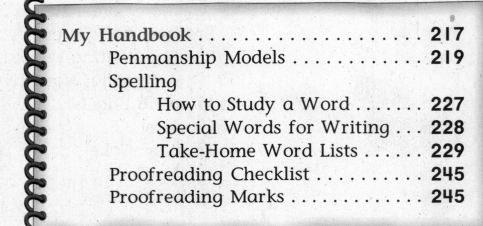

Punchouts

Name _____

Amazing Animals

Name some animals that you think are amazing.

Then list words that describe these animals.

Animal	Describing Words

Write a description that tells about your favorite amazing animal.

Use one of your describing words in the title.

_____

_____

_____

_____

_____

Name _____

Amazing Animals

Fill in the chart as you read the stories.

	What animals appear in this theme?	What amazing things do these animals do?
Officer Buckle and Gloria		
Ant		
The Great Ball Game		

Name _____

Missing Letters

**Finish each sentence by choosing a letter or letters from
each of the stars below. Print those letters on the line to
make a word that makes sense in the sentence.**

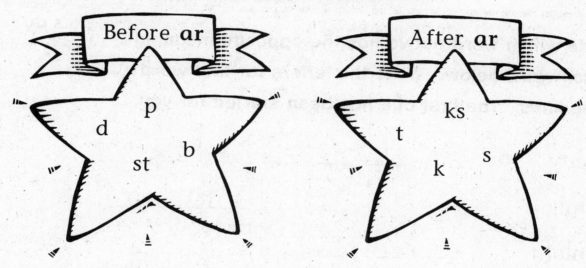

1. Gloria likes to run in the _____ar_____.

2. Gloria _____ar_____ every time she
   sees another dog.

3. Gloria does her _____ar_____ to
   teach safety tips.

4. When the children _____ar_____ to laugh,
   Gloria is happy.

5. Gloria is not afraid of the _____ar_____
   even when she is all alone.

6. Gloria is one of the _____ar_____ at school.

Theme 4: **Amazing Animals**   **3**

Name _____

Opposites Match

Word Bank

| short | more | forget | morning | before | forest | order |

**Decide which word above has the opposite meaning
of each word below. Write the letters for that word
on the lines. The first one has been started for you.**

1. city   f ___ ___ ___ |s| t

2. tall   ___ ___ |☐| ___ ___

3. night |☐| ___ ___ ___ ___ ___

4. after   ___ ___ ___ ___ |☐|

5. mess   ___ ___ |☐| ___ ___

6. less   ___ ___ |☐| ___

7. remember   ___ ___ ___ |☐| ___ ___

**In the boxes below, write the letters from the boxes
above. The words you make will answer the question.**

8. What did Officer Buckle say when he saw
Gloria on TV?

"That's |☐| |☐| |☐| |☐| |☐| |☐| |☐| !"

Name _____

Listen to the Tips

Finish each sentence with a word from the box.
You will use each word twice.

Word Bank

board	listen	told

1. Officer Buckle _____ the students
   about safety.

2. He asked them to _____ carefully.

3. They paid attention to everything he

   _____ them.

4. He wrote every safety tip on the _____.

5. He told them, "Always remember to _____
   to your parents!"

6. When he was finished, some students wrote

   their own safety tips on the _____.

Do not chew gum in school.

Say nice things to your big brother.

Watch your step getting on the bus.

Theme 4: **Amazing Animals**   5

Name _____

Safety Officer Words

Meanings

a. a group of people who watch and listen

b. a person who helps others follow the law

c. something you don't want to happen

d. freedom from danger

e. looking and listening with care

f. orders

Write the meaning from the box to match each word below.

1. accident _____

_____

2. attention _____

_____

3. audience _____

_____

4. commands _____

5. officer _____

_____

6. safety _____

Name _____

Drawing Conclusions Chart

As you read the story, use this chart to help you keep
track of what happens.

What I Think	My Clues
Officer Buckle's speeches are boring. (pages 22-23)	
Gloria makes the speeches more interesting. (pages 26-31)	
Officer Buckle doesn't know Gloria is doing tricks. (pages 27, 40, 43, 44)	
Officer Buckle and Gloria work best together. (pages 22, 45, 48, 50)	

Name _____

Check It Out

Each sentence has more than one ending. Read each ending. Put a ✔ next to the ending that tells what happened in the story.

1. When Officer Buckle gave his talks about safety,

   _____ children fell asleep.

   _____ everyone cheered.

2. The principal of Napville School wasn't listening when Officer Buckle said,

   _____ "Always stick with your buddy."

   _____ "Never stand on a swivel chair."

3. While watching television, Officer Buckle saw that

   _____ Gloria sat very still.

   _____ Gloria was the star.

4. Students loved Officer Buckle and Gloria

   _____ because they were a good team.

   _____ they told funny jokes.

Name _____

Drawing Conclusions

Read the story below. Then complete the chart on page 10.

Iguana Fun

Mrs. Persky's class was studying reptiles. So Ada's father brought his pet iguana Boris to school. When Ada's father walked into the classroom, Pedro ran to the back of the room. He stayed there the whole time.

Ada introduced her father and Boris to the class. Boris was dark green and had yellow eyes. Her father took Boris out of his cage. That made Evelyn hide under her desk. Ada said Boris was a nice iguana, but Evelyn would not move.

Ada's father said that Boris was almost fourteen inches long. He explained that this kind of iguana never gets longer than fourteen inches. Ada's father told the children not to worry about Boris. He said that iguanas move slowly after they have eaten. The children counted five orange rinds in the cage.

Mrs. Persky asked if she could hold Boris. Boris wrapped himself around her shoulders. Mrs. Persky talked softly to Boris. Some of the children petted Boris. Everyone thanked Ada's father for coming, except Pedro and Evelyn, that is.

Name _____

Drawing Conclusions continued

**After you've read the story "Iguana Fun," complete
the chart below.**

What I Read		What I Read		What This Tells Me
Boris is almost 14 inches long.	+	This kind of iguana never gets longer than 14 inches.	=	_____ _____ _____
An iguana is slow after it eats.	+	There are 5 orange rinds in the cage.	=	_____ _____ _____ _____
Pedro stays in the back of the room.	+	Evelyn hides under her desk.	=	_____ _____ _____ _____
Mrs. Persky lets Boris crawl on her shoulders.	+	Mrs. Persky talks softly to Boris.	=	_____ _____ _____ _____

Name _____

Amazing Dog

Use words from the box to finish the sentences about Gloria.

Word Bank

| capture | picture | attention | caption |
| action | station | mixture | motion |

1. Gloria is fun to watch when she's in _____.

2. She is a _____ of hard work and fun.

3. Gloria is always ready for _____.

4. Once she helped Officer Buckle _____ a robber.

5. The next day there was a _____ of her in the paper.

6. The _____ under the picture said that she was a brave dog.

7. Everyone at the police _____ loves Gloria.

8. Even the other dogs pay _____ to Gloria.

Name _____

Words with *ar*

► You hear the vowel + **r** sound in **car** and **start**. This sound is spelled **ar**.
► The word **warm** does not follow this pattern.

Write the Spelling Words that have the same vowel sound as *cart*.

cart

1. _____   7. _____

2. _____   8. _____

3. _____   9. _____

4. _____   10. _____

5. _____   11. _____

6. _____

On another sheet of paper, write a story about an amazing dog that you know. Use the Spelling Word *warm* in your story.

Name _____

Spelling Spree

Rhyme Time **Finish the sentences. Write Spelling Words to rhyme with the words in dark print.**

1. Gloria will **bark** at the _____.

2. The **card** says that it is not

   _____ to like Gloria.

3. Officer Buckle says to **start** being

   _____ about safety.

4. Stand **far** from a moving _____.

5. Would you like to be a **star** like Officer

   Buckle and Gloria _____?

1. car
2. smart
3. arm
4. park
5. yard
6. part
7. barn
8. hard
9. party
10. farm
11. are*
12. warm*

Unscramble the Letters **Unscramble each group of letters to make a Spelling Word. Write the words on the lines.**

6. n r b a _____

7. m r a _____

8. y r t a p _____

9. a f m r _____

10. a y d r _____

Name _____

Proofreading and Writing

Proofreading **Read the list of safety rules below.**
Circle the Spelling Words that are not spelled
correctly.

1. Before you cross the street, look to see if a care is coming.
2. In the pak, look out for people on bicycles.
3. Never touch a wharm iron.
4. Never swallow harrd candy whole.
5. Don't give the small purt of a toy to your baby sister.
6. Always be smahrt and safe!

Spelling Words

1. car
2. smart
3. arm
4. park
5. yard
6. part
7. barn
8. hard
9. party
10. farm
11. are*
12. warm*

Write each word you circled. Spell the word correctly.

1. _____   4. _____

2. _____   5. _____

3. _____   6. _____

Write Your Own Safety Rules **On another sheet of**
paper, write five safety rules you think are important.
Use Spelling Words from the list.

Name _____

Where Does It Belong?

Look at these dictionary entries. Write each entry word on the page where it belongs.

fail v. : not to succeed

bulldozer n. : a tractor with a blade in front

false adj. : not true

fade v. : to lose brightness or loudness

buddy n. : a good friend

bubble n. : a thin globe of air or gas

falcon n : a bird of prey

browse v. : to look for

brick / buck

_____

_____

face / fair

_____

_____

bucket / bully

_____

_____

fake / fame

_____

_____

Pronoun Show

► A **noun** names a person, a place, or a thing.
► A **pronoun** is a word that can take the place
of a noun.

**Rewrite each sentence. Replace the word or words in
dark print with the pronouns *she*, *he*, *it*, or *they*.**

1. **Gloria** likes to go to school.

_____

2. The **children** cheer when Gloria arrives.

_____

3. You can hear **the cheer** outside the school.

_____

4. When **Officer Buckle** starts to talk, the children
are quiet.

_____

5. **Officer Buckle and Gloria** put on a great show.

_____

Name _____

Pronoun Smart

Replace the underlined words with *she, he, it,* or *they.*
Write the new sentences on the lines.

1. On Saturday, <u>Officer Buckle</u> takes Gloria to
   the park.

   _____

   _____

2. Officer Buckle throws <u>a ball</u> for Gloria to catch.

   _____

3. <u>Gloria</u> runs after the big blue ball.

   _____

4. <u>Officer Buckle and Gloria</u> have a fun time together.

   _____

5. Then <u>Gloria</u> takes a nap under a tree.

   _____

Name _____

Pronoun News

Read the article from the school newspaper. Find places where a noun can be replaced with a pronoun. Draw a circle around the nouns that can be replaced.

Today Officer Buckle and Gloria came to our school. Officer Buckle is a safety officer and Gloria is a dog. Officer Buckle gave a safety talk. The safety talk was an important lesson for children. While Officer Buckle was talking, Gloria acted out the tips. Gloria is the funniest dog the students have ever seen. Don't miss their next visit!

Rewrite the article. Replace each noun you drew a circle around with a pronoun. Then read the article you have written to see if it makes sense.

_____

_____

_____

_____

_____

Name _____

Plan Ahead!

Plan a fun event. Use the form below to help you plan what you will write on an invitation.

Please Come!

My event will be

_____

The day and date of my event is

_____

The time of my event is

_____

*Remember to use A.M. or P.M. after the time.
My event will be at

_____

I will invite

_____

_____

Name _____

What Time Is It?

Read the paragraph below that tells what a day for a police officer and his dog, Spike, might be like. Then write the times that they did each thing in the schedule below. Remember to include A.M. or P.M. after the time.

At eight o'clock in the morning, the two go for a walk. At nine o'clock in the morning, they drive to Woodview Elementary School. They finish their safety talk at eleven o'clock. At twelve o'clock they stop in the park for lunch. Spike finds other dogs to play with. At one-thirty in the afternoon, they go to Smith Elementary School. Then at three o'clock they help children get safely on the school bus.

Schedule

_____ Go for walk

_____ Go to Woodview Elementary School

_____ Finish safety talk

_____ Lunch in park

_____ Go to Smith Elementary School

_____ Help children get on school bus

Name _____

Revising Your Research Report

Put a checkmark beside the sentences that describe your research report.

Superstar

☐ My report is informative and interesting.

☐ I used at least two sources to get information about my topic.

☐ I included many facts about my topic.

☐ I wrote the information in my own words.

☐ I used exact nouns.

☐ My research report has a good ending.

☐ There are few mistakes in my writing.

Rising Star

☐ I used one source of information.

☐ I need to include more facts about my topic.

☐ I did not tell the information in my own words.

☐ My report could be more interesting.

☐ I need to use more exact nouns.

☐ My report does not have a good ending.

☐ There are many mistakes in my writing.

Name _____

Using Exact Nouns

**Read the sentences. Use a word from the box to
change the underlined noun in each sentence to an
exact noun.**

> hot dogs   corn   dog   apples   coat   cows

1. I fed my <u>pet</u>. _____

2. My mom likes to eat <u>fruit</u>. _____

3. I could smell the <u>meat</u> cooking.

   _____

4. She helped Tim put on his <u>things</u>.

   _____

5. I saw <u>animals</u> in the barn. _____

6. We like to grow <u>food</u> in our garden. _____

Special Words for Writing

These Spelling Words are words that you use in your writing. Look carefully at how they are spelled. Write the missing letters in the Spelling Words below. Use the words in the box to help you.

1. done
2. girl
3. found
4. into
5. your
6. around
7. back
8. one
9. some
10. two
11. once
12. I'll

1. f _____ n d

2. y o ___ r

3. g _____ l

4. b _____ k

5. o ___ e

6. I' _____

7. s _____ e

8. d _____ e

9. t ___ o

10. i ___ t ___

11. a ___ o u ___ d

12. o _____ e

Write the Spelling Words on the lines below.

_____   _____   _____

_____   _____   _____

_____   _____   _____

_____

Name _____

Spelling Spree

Write a Spelling Word to complete the sentences.

1. The little ____ went to the zoo.
2. She saw ____ black bears eating fish.
3. Then, ____ chimpanzees jumped up and down.
4. ____ huge hippo was swimming in the water.
5. Snakes were crawling all ____.
6. "I'll come ____ to see the mountain goats," she said.
7. She ran ____ the penguin's house.
8. " ____ bus is waiting," shouted the zookeeper.

Spelling Words

1. done
2. girl
3. found
4. into
5. your
6. around
7. back
8. one
9. some
10. two
11. once
12. I'll

1. _____   5. _____

2. _____   6. _____

3. _____   7. _____

4. _____   8. _____

9. Which Spelling Word is a contraction? _____

10. Which Spelling Word means to find something?

_____

Name _____

Proofreading and Writing

Proofreading Find and circle misspelled Spelling Words in this report. Then write the words.

Spelling Words

The earthworm is yor garden's helper. Earthworms crawl arund underground. They dig tunnels by eating, digging, stretching, and squeezing. Ones they mix up all the dirt, the roots of plants can grow.

Earthworms need to stay moist to breathe. They breathe through their skin. They do not come out during the day because they might dry up. They come out at night to find something to eat. When they are dun, they crawl bak into the ground.

Spelling Words

1. done
2. girl
3. found
4. into
5. your
6. around
7. back
8. one
9. some
10. two
11. once
12. I'll

1. _____ 3. _____ 5. _____

2. _____ 4. _____

Write an Animal Note Write a note on another sheet of paper. Tell about an animal you like. Be sure to include some facts about that animal. Start your note with *Dear* and end it with *Your friend,*. Use as many Spelling Words as you can.

Ant

Phonics Skill Words with
nd, nt, mp, ng, nk

Letter Changes

Change the dark letter in each word to make a new word. Each word should end with the letters *nd, nt, mp, ng,* or *nk*. The clues will help you.

1. kin**d**   not queen   _____

2. ca**m**e   place for tents   _____

3. thin**g**   you do this
            with your brain   _____

4. **p**anes   piece of clothing _____

5. **c**hime   small ape   _____

6. sin**g**   something to
            wash dishes in   _____

7. la**n**e   not water   _____

On the lines below write 3 sentences. Use one of the new words you made in each sentence.

8. _____

_____

_____

Name _____

Ant

Phonics Skill Structural Analysis: Base Words and Endings -s, -es, -ies (nouns)

Ant Funnies

Write the base word and ending for each word in dark type.

1. Let me tell you about the queen ant. She likes to read **stories** to the other ants.

   base word _____ ending _____

2. She likes to eat on silver **dishes**.

   base word _____ ending _____

3. She keeps all her food in wooden **boxes**.

   base word _____ ending _____

4. Her best friend is the queen of the **flies**.

   base word _____ ending _____

Now read the sentences below. Make the underlined words mean more than one by adding -s or -es or by changing the y to -ies. Write the new words on the lines.

5. Ants live in _____. colony

6. Army ants live in _____. jungle

7. Larvae are like ant _____. baby

8. Ants have strong _____. body

Copyright © Houghton Mifflin Company. All rights reserved.

Theme 4: **Amazing Animals** 27

Name _____

Fancy Ants

Word Bank

| between | care | weigh |

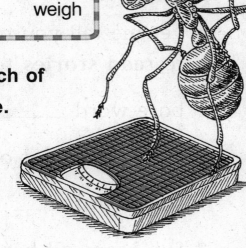

Find the words in the box that rhyme with each of the words below. Write the words on the line.

1. bean _____

2. hair _____

3. stay _____

Use a word from the box to finish each question.
Then read the answer to each question.

4. Who can take _____ of a hungry ant?

     the ant's AuNT

5. How do you _____ an ant?

     you cAN'T

6. What does an ant eat as a snack

_____ meals?

     green plANTs

Name _____

How Are They Alike?

Read the questions. Use words from the box to write sentences that answer the questions. The first one has been done for you.

Vocabulary

- antennae
- larvae
- fungus
- cocoons
- colonies
- tunnels

1. Where do ants, prairie dogs, and termites live in groups?

   They live in colonies.

2. What underground place do ants, cars, and gophers travel through?

   _____

3. What do ants, moths, and other insects have on their heads?

   _____

4. What are mushrooms, molds, and mildew that grow in damp places?

   _____

5. What do silkworms, ants, and butterflies live in as they change and grow?

   _____

6. What are young butterflies, ants, or moths called?

   _____

Text Organization Chart

As you read the story, use this chart to help you keep track of what you learn about ants.

Main Idea	Details
Ants make anthills. (pages 64–65)	
Ants have antennae. (pages 66–67)	
Ants work together. (pages 68-69)	
Some ants are called leafcutter ants. (pages 72-73)	

Name _____

About the Story

Look at the picture. Then finish the sentence beside the picture.

1. When you see an anthill, you know that

_____

_____

2. An ant uses its antennae to

_____

_____

3. The ant carries leaves because

_____

_____

4. The ant is "milking" the caterpillar because

_____

_____

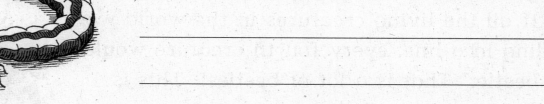 Theme 4: **Amazing Animals**   **31**

Name _____

Text Organization

Read the article below. Then complete the chart on page 33.

Amazing Beetles

Beetles may be the kings of insects.
Beetles have lived on Earth longer than any
other insect. There are more beetles than any
other kind of insect.

Almost 400,000 kinds of beetles live on
Earth. You need a magnifying glass to see the
smallest beetle. The biggest beetles live in the
jungle. They are six inches long. That's longer
than your hand! Some beetles have shiny green
bodies. Some are plain and brown. You may
have held one kind of beetle in your hand — the
ladybug.

People do many things with beetles. People
with gardens buy boxes of ladybugs. Ladybugs
are good for gardens. They eat insects that hurt
plants. Some people make jewelry from fancy
green beetles. Other people keep beetles for pets.
In some parts of the world, beetles are food. People
eat the beetles.

If all the living creatures in the world were
standing in a line, every fourth creature would
be a beetle. That is a lot of beetles! This is
why the beetle is called the king of insects.

Name _____

Text Organization continued

After you've read the article *Amazing Beetles*, complete the chart below.

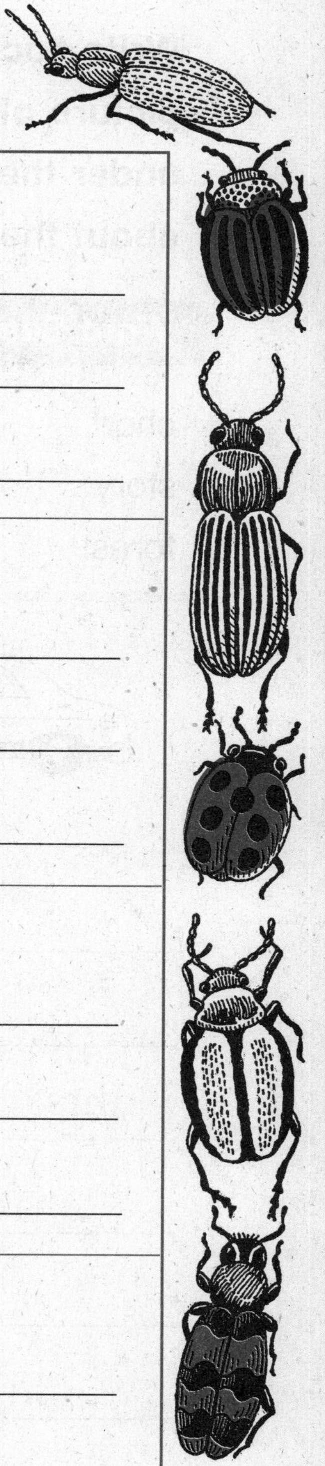

Paragraph 1
Main Idea: _____
Details: _____
_____
Paragraph 2
Main Idea: _____
Details: _____
_____
Paragraph 3
Main Idea: _____
Details: _____
_____
Paragraph 4
Main Idea: _____
Details: _____

Start Sorting!

Write each word in the box with the letters *ar* under the picture of the car. Write each word with the letters *or* under the picture of the fork. Then use what you know about the sounds for *ar* and *or* to read each word.

Word Bank

chart	farmer	harder	more
story	card	short	part
forest	fort	sharp	horse

Car

_____

_____

_____

_____

_____

Fork

_____

_____

_____

_____

_____

for

park

Name _____

Words That End with *nd*, *ng*, or *nk*

► You hear the sounds of **n** and **d** in words that end with the consonants **nd**.

► You may not hear the sound of **n** in words that end with the consonants **ng** or **nk**.

1. king
2. thank
3. hand
4. sing
5. send
6. think
7. bring
8. bang
9. end
10. thing
11. and
12. long

Write the Spelling Words that end with *nd*.

pond

_____   _____

_____   _____

Write the Spelling Words that end with *ng*.

ring

_____   _____

_____   _____

_____   _____

Write the Spelling Words that end with *nk*.

skunk

_____   _____

Name _____

Spelling Spree

Code Breaker Use the code to find each Spelling
Word. Write the Spelling Word on the line.

◯ = nd   ▢ = nk   △ = ng

thi▢ = _____   ki△ = _____

se◯ = _____   ha◯ = _____

si△ = _____   ba△ = _____

1. king
2. thank
3. hand
4. sing
5. send
6. think
7. bring
8. bang
9. end
10. thing
11. and
12. long

Word Search Find the Spelling Word hidden in
each sentence. Circle the letters that make the
word. Then write the Spelling Word. The first one
has been done for you.

1. One rai(sin)goes on each cookie. _____sing_____

2. An ant can do amazing things with its

   antennae. _____

3. When does an ant take a break? _____

4. Ants can even climb ringing bells. _____

5. Ants live where the melon grows. _____

Name _____

Proofreading and Writing

Proofreading Circle four Spelling Words that are
incorrect. Then write each word correctly.

April 4 Today I watched six ants carry a
grasshopper. They must be very strong. What a
ting to do. That would be like six men carrying an
elephant!

April 8 I put my hande on a fire-ant nest by
accident. The stings really hurt, but my dad helped.
He put honey on them!

April 9 Today I read about the queen ant. I wonder
if there is a king. I don't thenk so.

April 12 I visited the nature museum today. A
man there who studies ants showed me around.
Tomorrow I will write to thaink him for the
great visit.

Spelling Words

1. king
2. thank
3. hand
4. sing
5. send
6. think
7. bring
8. bang
9. end
10. thing
11. and
12. long

1. _____   3. _____

2. _____   4. _____

Write a Report Read more about ants. Write a short report
on a separate piece of paper. Use the Spelling Words.

Choose the Best Word

home: house, cave, hive
mountain: cliff, hill
shorten: chop, clip

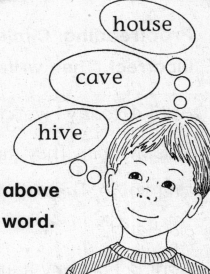

**Read each sentence. Use the word from the list above
to replace each underlined word. Write the new word.**

1. The anthill was close to the bees' <u>home</u>.

   _____

2. The eagle has its nest on a <u>mountain</u> where

   people never hike. _____

3. In the bear's <u>home</u> we found many bones.

   _____

4. I will <u>shorten</u> this carrot for the salad.

   _____

5. It was easy to climb the <u>mountain</u>. _____

6. My mother wants to <u>shorten</u> my dog's nails.

   _____

Name _____

Who Owns Something?

► A possessive noun is a word that
shows ownership.

► An apostrophe and **s** are added to the end
of the noun to show that it is possessive.

**Read the sentences below. Decide who or what owns
something. Then rewrite each sentence to show
ownership. Remember to add the apostrophe. The
first one has been done for you.**

1. These are the antennae of the ant.
   These are the ant's antennae.
   _____

2. The queen of the colony is very important.

   _____

3. Workers care for the eggs of the queen.

   _____

4. The job of the worker is also to find food.

   _____

5. The home of the aphid is near the colony.

   _____

6. Ants are the favorite food of the anteater.

   _____

Name _____

Match It!

Read each group of words below.

> **Word Bank**
>
> queen's eggs   colony's tunnel
>
> worker's leaf   tree's roots

Now draw a line from pictures under the letter _A_ to pictures under the letter _B_ to show the meaning of each phrase above.

A   B

 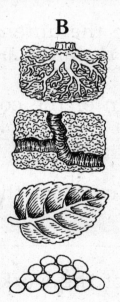

Now write two sentences. Use one of the phrases at the top of the page in each of your sentences.

_____

_____

_____

Name _____

Ants in the Yard

Read Dora's story. She forgot to add apostrophes to show ownership. Circle the words that need apostrophes.

There are ants in my grandmothers yard. The ant colony is by the trees roots. I like to watch the ants. They are so busy. An ants antennae move all the time. The ants march in long lines. They carry food back to the colony. I once saw them carrying a grasshoppers wing. Another time I saw an ant with a cookie crumb. That was my cookie! That ants dinner was going to be very sweet!

On the lines below, write the words you circled with the words that show what is owned. Remember to add apostrophes to show ownership.

1. _____   4. _____

2. _____   5. _____

3. _____

Name _____

Poem Words

Use the two charts to help you get started writing a poem. Write a topic that interests you in each circle. Then list words that go with that topic. For each topic, choose two of those words and list words that rhyme with them. Try to choose rhyming words that will fit with your topic.

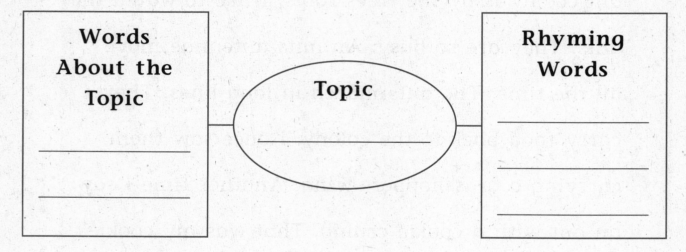

Name _____

I or Me?

Read the letter below. The word *I* or the word *me* belongs in each blank space. Rewrite the letter using the words *I* and *me* correctly.

Dear Jamie,

    Yesterday my dad and ____ went to the nature museum. There was a giant ant farm there. Dad and ____ watched the ants for almost an hour. Then the museum guide took Dad and ____ on a tour around the museum. We had so much fun. If we go again, would you like to go with Dad and ____?

               Your friend,

               Brett

_____

_____

_____

_____

_____

_____

Name _____

A Walk Outside

Write the word from the box that completes each sentence.

Word Bank

| low | toad | coat | crow | croak | willow |

1. Ben put on his _____ .

2. He walked by a tall _____ tree.

3. He watched a _____ fly out of a tree.

4. It swooped _____ to the ground.

5. Then Ben saw a _____ hopping by the pond.

6. A frog gave a loud _____ as the toad hopped by.

Now write each word under the animal that has the same vowel spelling.

oa

ow

_____   _____

_____   _____

_____   _____

Write a Letter

Read this letter that Crane wrote to Bear.

Dear Bear,

   Not long <u>ago</u>, you and I were friends. We would play <u>in</u> the <u>field</u> together. Now we are angry with each other. You play alone in <u>half</u> of the meadow, while I play in the other half. It feels like we are at <u>war</u>. I think we should talk about the problem. What do you think?

                              Sincerely,
                              Crane

Pretend you are Bear. Write an answer to Crane. Use each of the underlined words in your answer.

Dear Crane,

_____

_____

_____

_____

_____

                              Sincerely,
                              Bear

Name _____

Replacing Words

Read each sentence. Replace each word in dark print with a word from the box. Write the letters of that word in the spaces.

> ## Vocabulary
>
> accept   advantage   argument   penalty   quarrel

1. Two bear cubs had a big **disagreement**.

   __ __ __ __ __ __ __ __

2. One cub had an **edge** because he was bigger.

   __ __ __ __ __ __ __ __ __

3. That cub thought that bigger was better.
   The other cub did not **agree** that this was true.

   __ __ __ __ __ __

4. Mother Bear heard the **disagreement**.

   __ __ __ __ __ __ __ __

5. She said, "There will be a **punishment** if you two cubs do not settle this fight."

   __ __ __ __ __ __ __

On another sheet of paper, write an ending to the story. Tell how you think the cubs will solve the argument.

Name _____

Cause-Effect Chart

As you read the story, complete the chart below.

What Happens ➡	Why It Happens
(page 92) The Birds and Animals have a big _____.	
(page 94) The Birds and Animals decide to have a _____.	
(page 96) _____ is left out of the game.	
(Page 104) Bat wins the game for the _____.	
(page 108) Birds fly _____ each winter.	
(page 109) Bat comes flying every day at _____.	

Theme 4: **Amazing Animals**   47

Name _____

Ball Game Clues

Use the clues to complete the puzzle.

1. The Animals and the Birds had a big _____.
2. The _____ thought they were better because they had teeth.
3. The Birds thought they were better because they had _____.
4. They decided to play a ball _____ to decide who was better.
5. Little _____ had both wings and teeth.
6. Bat made the winning _____.
7. The Birds had to fly _____ each winter because they had lost.

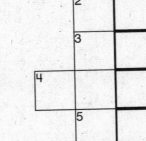

Write the letters from the boxes in dark print to answer this question.

8. Which team won the ball game?

_____ _____ _____ _____ _____ _____

Name _____

Cause ➡ Effect

Read the fable. Then complete the chart on page 50.

The Lion and the Mouse

A lion lay asleep in the sun. A little mouse darted across the lion's paw. The lion woke up. He grabbed the tiny mouse and opened his great, big mouth.

Just as the lion was about to eat him, the mouse cried, "I didn't mean to wake you up, kind lion. Please don't eat me! I will always be thankful. Someday, maybe I will be able to help you."

The lion roared with laughter. He said, "What could you ever do for me? I am so big! You are so small." But the lion put the little mouse down, because the mouse had made him laugh. The mouse scampered away into the grass.

Several weeks passed. The mouse was looking for food when he heard loud, angry roars. The mouse was scared, but he went to see who was making the terrible noise. He found the lion caught in a hunter's net. Quickly, the mouse ran to the net. He used his sharp teeth to chew the threads. The lion was soon free.

The lion said, "Thank you, little mouse. Sometimes the smallest friends are the biggest friends."

Name _____

Cause Effect continued

After you have read the fable about the lion and the mouse, complete the chart below.

Cause		Effect
1. The mouse ran across the lion's paw.	➡	_____ _____
2. The mouse made the lion laugh.	➡	_____ _____
3. _____ _____	➡	The mouse was scared. He went to see what was making the noise.
4. _____ _____	➡	The lion got out of the net.
5. The lion was free.	➡	_____ _____

Name _____

Tongue Twister Sentences

**Write the three rhyming words in
each sentence.**

1. The pig spilled pink ink in the sink.

   _____ _____ _____

2. The tiger sent a tent that was bent.

   _____ _____ _____

3. The band got a hand from animals sitting in the stand.

   _____ _____ _____

4. The cat likes to tramp on the lamp at camp.

   _____ _____ _____

5. The skunk fell off the trunk and went kerplunk!

   _____ _____ _____

6. The goat with the long beard played the wrong song.

   _____ _____ _____

Name _____

The Long *o* Sound?

Most of the Spelling Words have the long **o**
sound spelled **o**, **oa**, or **ow**.

    Example: go, boat, slow

► The word **toe** is special. The vowels **oe**
   spell the long **o** sound in **toe**.

► The word **do** is special. The vowel **o** does
   not spell the long **o** sound in **do**.

Write each Spelling Word under the correct column.

1. boat
2. cold
3. road
4. blow
5. gold
6. old
7. load
8. snow
9. hold
10. most
11. toe*
12. do*

long o sound spelled o	long o sound spelled oa
_____	_____
_____	_____
_____	_____
_____	

      long o sound
      spelled ow

     _____

     _____

**Write the special words that have a star next to
them. Circle the word that has the long o sound.**

_____   _____

Name _____

Spelling Spree

Word Games Think how the words in each group are alike. Write the missing Spelling Words.

Spelling Words

1. boat
2. cold
3. road
4. blow
5. gold
6. old
7. load
8. snow
9. hold
10. most
11. toe*
12. do*

1. street, path, _____

2. silver, copper, _____

3. rain, sleet, _____

4. grab, grip, _____

5. finger, nose, _____

6. all, some, _____

7. chilly, cool, _____

8. ship, raft, _____

9. fill, pack, _____

10. make, act, _____

Theme 4: **Amazing Animals**   53

Name _____

Proofreading and Writing

Proofreading Circle the four Spelling Words in this story that are not spelled correctly. Write each of the words correctly on the lines.

1. boat
2. cold
3. road
4. blow
5. gold
6. old
7. load
8. snow
9. hold
10. most
11. toe*
12. do*

The wind began to blo harder. The air was getting very cold. The birds flew faster. They wanted to get to the ocean before the snoe came. It wouldn't be long now. In fact, there was the water ahead. Soon the birds saw a boat below. All they had to dow was follow the oald bird. He had traveled the path for many years.

_____   _____

_____   _____

Writing Sentences Some birds fly thousands of miles to get to a warmer place. What would it be like to be one of those birds? Write about it on a separate sheet of paper. Use Spelling Words from the list.

Name _____

Dictionary Word Match

Most dictionary entries include a picture, an entry word, the meaning of the word, and a sample sentence. Look at the example below. Then read each entry and decide what is missing. Add that part to the entry.

Example

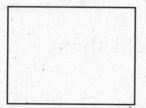

walrus A large sea animal that is related to seals. This mammal has a thick hide, two tusks, and flippers. *A walrus dived into the sea.*

web Thin threads put together in a special way by a spider. *The spider worked all night to spin a web.*

whisker: _____

_____

The baby tried to pull the cat's whisker.

_____ The part that birds, insects, and airplanes use to fly. *The baby bird hurt its wing when it fell out of the nest.*

Name _____

Who Owns Something?

► A plural noun means more than one and
  usually ends in **s.**
► A possessive plural noun shows that something
  belongs to more than one person, animal,
  or thing. These nouns usually end in **-s'.**
► Some plural nouns, such as **children**
  and **mice**, do not end in **-s.** To form
  the possessive of these nouns, add **-'s.**

**Read each sentence. Decide if the underlined word
should end with *-s' or -'s* . Write the correct word
and ending on the line.**

<u>players</u>   1. The _____ coach told them
                to kick the ball toward the goal.

<u>referees</u>   2. The _____ whistles blew
                when the ball went into the net.

<u>parents</u>   3. The _____ cheers could
                be heard across the field.

<u>children</u>   4. One person handed out all the

                _____ medals.

<u>Smiths</u>   5. The winning team went to the

                _____ home for a party.

Name _____

Nouns That Belong

► A plural noun usually ends in **-s**.

► A possessive plural noun shows that something belongs to more than one person, animal, or thing. These nouns usually end in **-s'**.

► Some plural nouns, such as **children** and **mice**, do not end in **-s**. To form the possessive, add **-'s**.

Rewrite each sentence. Use the correct possessive noun.

1. The  ears are floppy.
rabbits

_____

2. The  babies are hungry.
birds

_____

3. The  cage is dirty.
mice

_____

4. The  wool is soft.
sheep

_____

Theme 4: **Amazing Animals**   57

Name _____

More Than One

Mrs. Howard wrote a list of chores for her pet shop. She made some mistakes. Read the list. Decide whether an ' or an 's should be added to the animal name in each sentence. Rewrite the sentence.

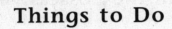

Things to Do

1. Mix the dogs food in their bowls.

   _____

2. Clean out the cats boxes.

   _____

3. Fill the mice water bottles.

   _____

4. Get a helper to put the puppies toys in the pen.

   _____

5. Wash the walls of the fish tanks.

   _____

Name _____

In the News

Use the picture to gather information for writing an article about
the baseball game. Answer the questions.

Welcome to Oklahoma City for the Little League Baseball Finals June 13-16

SCORE
BEARS 3   TIGERS 2

Question	Information
Who?	_____
What?	_____
When?	_____
Where?	_____
Why?	_____
How?	_____

Use the information you wrote to write a news article about the
game on another sheet of paper. Remember to add details that
will catch a reader's interest.

Name _____

Add Details to the Story

Read the news article. Rewrite sentences on the lines below. Add details that will make your sentences more interesting.

Zoo Opens New Snake House

The zoo opened a new snake house. People came to see it on Friday. Visitors found all kinds of snakes. A zookeeper fed the snakes. Mr. Diaz, the zoo manager, said, "People have always wanted to see bigger snakes. We were lucky to have a person donate the money for this exhibit." The zoo is open every day.

1. The zoo opened a new snake house.

   _____

2. People came to see it on Friday.

   _____

3. Visitors found all kinds of snakes.

   _____

4. A zookeeper fed the snakes.

   _____

5. The zoo is open every day.

   _____

Name _____

Vocabulary

Use what you have learned about taking tests to help you choose the correct word for a sentence. This practice will help you when you take this kind of test.

Read the two sentences. Each sentence has a numbered blank. Choose the word from each list that best completes the sentence.

Ants live together in groups called ____1____. These groups live in ____2____ under the ground.

1 ⚪ parties   **2** ⚪ corners

   ⚪ colonies   ⚪ rocks

   ⚪ nests   ⚪ caves

   ⚪ flocks   ⚪ tunnels

When you see an ____3____ above ground, you know ants are living under it. Ants may live for many ____4____ in the same place.

3 ⚪ apple   **4** ⚪ weeks

   ⚪ puddle   ⚪ years

   ⚪ anthill   ⚪ minutes

   ⚪ sidewalk   ⚪ days

Name _____

Vocabulary continued

An ant has two long ____5____ on its head.
They help the ant ____6____ food and find its way
home.

5 ○ twigs   6 ○ find

   ○ feathers   ○ eat

   ○ antennae   ○ carry

   ○ wings   ○ drop

The one biggest ant is called the ____7____.
This ant lays all the ____8____.

7 ○ aunt   8 ○ food

   ○ queen   ○ chicks

   ○ uncle   ○ eggs

   ○ king   ○ logs

Ants are very ____9____. They can carry
things that are much ____10____ than they are.

9 ○ weak   10 ○ bigger

   ○ strong   ○ cleaner

   ○ silly   ○ greener

   ○ pretty   ○ slower

Name _____

Spelling Review

Write Spelling Words from the list to answer the questions.

1–5. Which words have the vowel + **r** sounds in **car**?

1. _____   4. _____

2. _____   5. _____

3. _____

6–12. Which words end in **nd**, **ng**, or **nk**?

6. _____   10. _____

7. _____   11. _____

8. _____   12. _____

9. _____

13–20. Which words have the long **o** sound?

13. _____   17. _____

14. _____   18. _____

15. _____   19. _____

16. _____   20. _____

Spelling Words

1. cold
2. party
3. think
4. boat
5. thank
6. smart
7. road
8. sing
9. hand
10. load
11. farm
12. thing
13. blow
14. most
15. send
16. park
17. bring
18. snow
19. hold
20. yard

Name _____

Spelling Spree

Letter Swap Change the last letter of each word
to make a Spelling Word. Write the Spelling
Words.

1. fare _____

2. hole _____

3. blob _____

4. yarn _____

1. think
2. blow
3. yard
4. park
5. cold
6. sing
7. thank
8. farm
9. hold
10. send

Hide and Seek Circle the six Spelling Words
hidden in the snake. Then write the words.

drthinkfetcoldwrzsingpxpluthankmsendwertrparkqwx

5. _____   8. _____

6. _____   9. _____

7. _____   10. _____

Proofreading and Writing

Proofreading Circle four Spelling Words that are wrong below. Write each word correctly.

Leo the Lion had a bright red bote.

He liked to row. On some days, Leo would

bringe food to eat. He took a lowd

of lion snacks. Wasn't he a smartt lion?

Spelling Words

1. bring
2. smart
3. snow
4. most
5. boat
6. hand
7. road
8. load
9. party
10. thing

1. _____   3. _____

2. _____   4. _____

Finish the Story Write Spelling Words to complete this story.

It was the day of Dan's 5. _____. There was a

lot of 6. _____ on the ground. Dan wanted to

clear the 7. _____. His dad said, "There's one

8. _____ we can do. Give me a helping 9.

_____." Soon 10. _____ of the

sidewalk was cleared.

Write a Story On another sheet of paper, write a story about an animal. Use the Spelling Review Words.

Name _____

Family Time

Create a funny family story. First, fill in items 1–6. Then use those words to complete the story.

1. Name a person in your family. _____

2. Name a favorite family food. _____

3. Write a verb that names an action that

    happened in the past. _____

4. Name an object that you find indoors. _____

5. Name an animal. _____

One day _____ and I decided to make
                              1

_____ for the entire family. It was a lot
        2

of work.

_____ _____ everything into
        1   3

a big bowl. It was very hard to stir. We had to

mix it with a _____ .
                         4

   After all that work, nobody wanted to eat

the _____ , so we had to feed it to our pet
        2

_____ . Next time, we'll use a recipe!
        5

Name _____

Family Time

Fill in the chart as you read the stories.

	What family members appear in this theme?	What do family members do together in this theme?
Brothers and Sisters		
Jalapeño Bagels		
Carousel		
Thunder Cake		

Name _____

What Goes with What?

Word Bank

summer	October	number
November	letter	winter

Decide which two words in the list above go with the word in each circle. Write those words in the boxes connected to the circle.

seasons

summer

seasons

1. _____

2. _____

things you write

3. _____

4. _____

months of the year

5. _____

6. _____

Name _____

Word Play

Word Bank

| trouble | middle | uncle |

Draw a line from each word to the meaning of the word.

Words

1. trouble
2. middle
3. uncle

Meanings

center

your mother or father's brother

difficulty

Unscramble each group of letters to make a word.

4. beorult _____

5. ldiemd _____

6. nceul _____

Write the words from the box that rhyme with the words in dark print.

7. **double** _____

8. **fiddle** _____

Name _____

Bubbling Words

Circle the word that best completes each sentence.

1. Our family went to the hospital to see my aunt's ___ baby.

   newborn   distract   pest

2. The ___ in my class look just alike.

   distract   twins   newborn

3. Fred's ___ brother is learning to drive a car.

   teenage   pest   newborn

4. Rhonda will try to ___ the baby with a toy.

   twins   teenage   distract

On another sheet of paper, write 4 sentences. Use one of the words you circled in each sentence.

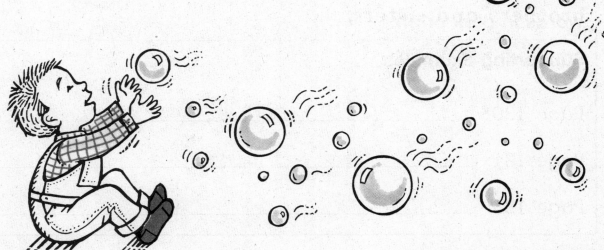

Name _____

Generalizations Chart

Complete the chart below as you read *Brothers and Sisters*. Complete the generalization sentences and find examples to support each generalization.

Generalization
A new baby _____ life for everyone in the family.
Supporting Examples
Page 128: _____
Page 129: _____
Page 130: _____

Generalization
Older children _____ younger brothers and sisters.
Supporting Examples
Page 130: _____
Page 131: _____
Page 133: _____

Name _____

Name _____

Taking Turns

Read the story. Then complete the chart on page 75.

Amy and Luke are sister and brother. They take turns when they play games. Sometimes it is easy to take turns. Sometimes it is not.

Dad asks the children if they want to go to the store. Amy and Luke race to the car. They each try to be first to get in the front seat. Dad asks whose turn it is to ride up front. Amy and Luke both say, "Mine!" But Dad says it is Amy's turn.

When Luke and Amy get home from the store, they want to watch a television show. They argue about who gets to choose. Dad asks whose turn it is. Luke and Amy both say, "Mine!" Dad tells Luke to pick the show.

After the show, Mom says she will read them a story. The children want her to read different stories. Mom asks whose turn it is to pick. Luke and Amy both say, "Mine!" Mom says it is Amy's turn.

When Mom finishes the story, she asks whose turn it is to wash the dishes. Amy says, "His!" Luke says, "Hers!" Mom and Dad laugh.

Name _____

Taking Turns continued

After you've read the story, complete the chart below.

Write sentences that will support the generalization.

Generalization:

Brothers and sisters have to take turns.

Supporting Information

1. _____

_____

2. _____

_____

3. _____

_____

4. _____

_____

5. _____

_____

Name _____

Word Groups

Read the words below. Think how the words in each group are alike. Write the missing *oa* or *ow* word that will fit in each group.

ow		**oa**	
crow	snowing	goat	road
throw	bowl	boat	coat
yellow		groaning	

1. plate, cup, _____

2. highway, street, _____

3. robin, blue jay, _____

4. raining, sleeting, _____

5. moaning, crying, _____

6. train, car, _____

7. green, blue, _____

8. horse, pig, _____

9. catch, toss, _____

10. jacket, sweater, _____

Name _____

Spelling Beats

Write the Spelling Words, dividing them into syllables or beats. Use a dictionary if you need help.

1. flower   _____ _____

2. water   _____ _____

3. under   _____ _____

4. over   _____ _____

5. better   _____ _____

6. sister   _____ _____

7. brother   _____ _____

8. mother   _____ _____

9. father   _____ _____

10. after   _____ _____

Name _____

Spelling Clues

**Write the Spelling Word
for each clue.**

Spelling Words

1. flower
2. water
3. under
4. over
5. better
6. sister
7. brother
8. mother
9. father
10. after

1. the opposite of brother

_____

2. another word for blossom

_____

3. the opposite of over

_____

4. rhymes with mother

_____

5. the opposite of worse

_____

6. something to drink _____

7. the opposite of before _____

8. another word for mom _____

9. rhymes with clover _____

10. another word for dad _____

mother

father

brother

sister

Name _____

Proofreading and Writing

**Proofreading Circle four Spelling Words that
are spelled wrong in this postcard. Then write
each word correctly.**

Dear Grandma,

We are having a great camping trip. Dad
put our tent udner a big tree. We can hear
the watr flow ovver the rocks in a nearby
stream. Last night Mom cooked hot dogs.
Today we went on a hike. I wanted to pick a
flower, but Mom said it was bedder to leave
the plant alone.

                    Love,

                    Pat

Spelling Words

1. flower
2. water
3. under
4. over
5. better
6. sister
7. brother
8. mother
9. father
10. after

1. _____   3. _____

2. _____   4. _____

**Write a Postcard On a separate piece of paper,
write a postcard to someone in your family. Include
some of your Spelling Words in the message on
your postcard.**

Name _____

Growing Words

**Write the words that are in the word families for *wonder*,
hard, *love*, and *sleep* on the lines under each word.**

Word Bank

hardest	loving	sleeps	lovely	hardly
sleepy	wonderful	wonders	wondering	loves

w o n d e r

1. _____

2. _____

3. _____

l o v e

6. _____

7. _____

8. _____

h a r d

4. _____

5. _____

s l e e p

9. _____

10. _____

Name _____

Lasso the Verbs

► A verb tells what someone or something does.

► A verb can name an action such as **run**, **talk**, and **smile**.

► A verb can also name an activity that cannot be seen such as **hear**, **think**, and **worry**.

Circle the verb in each sentence.

1. Teri hugs her little sister.

2. The baby takes a nap every day.

3. Sometimes Caleb's little brother cries.

4. The baby's toy plays music.

5. Tony has a big brother and a little sister.

6. Jared put his toys in the closet.

7. Shameka and Ann race to the corner of the yard.

8. Patsy and David climb on the monkey bars.

9. The children draw pictures in the sand.

10. The waves splash water onto the children's feet.

Name _____

Teddy Bear Verbs

► A verb tells what someone or something does. A verb can name an action such as **run**, **talk**, and **smile**.

► A verb can also name an activity that cannot be seen. The words **hear**, **think**, and **worry** are verbs.

Color the puzzle pieces with verbs brown.

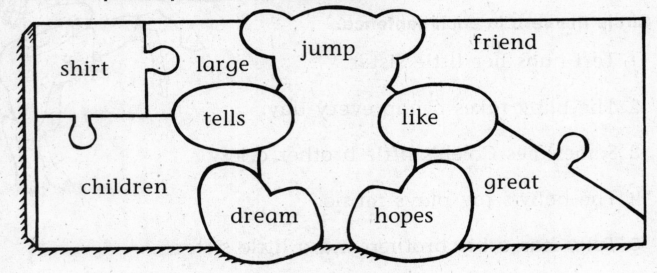

Write a sentence using each of the following verbs.

1. learn _____

2. have _____

3. talk _____

4. run _____

5. climb _____

Name _____

Using Exciting Verbs

Read the journal entry below. As you read, think about words that you could use in place of the underlined verbs.

Monday

My alarm did not ring this morning. I <u>got</u> up and saw I was late. I <u>cleaned</u> my face and brushed my teeth. I put on some clean clothes. I <u>went</u> downstairs. I quickly <u>had</u> my breakfast. My Dad <u>said</u>, "Hurry! The bus is coming." I <u>got</u> my backpack. I <u>went</u> to the bus stop as fast as I could. The bus <u>came</u> down the street just as I arrived.

Now fill in the blanks with verbs that will make the writing clearer and more exciting.

Monday

My alarm did not ring this morning. I _____

up and saw I was late. I _____ my face and

brushed my teeth. I put on some clean clothes. I _____

downstairs. I quickly _____ my breakfast. My dad

_____, "Hurry! The bus is coming." I

_____ my backpack. I _____ to the

bus stop as fast as I could. The bus _____ down

the street just as I arrived.

Name _____

What Do You Think?

Write an opinion in the box. Then write reasons for your opinion. Give details or examples that will support your reasons.

Opinion: _____

_____

Reason 1: _____

_____

Detail or Example 1:

_____

Detail or Example 2:

_____

Reason 2: _____

_____

Detail or Example 1:

_____

Detail or Example 2:

_____

Name _____

Your Opinion

Rewrite each opinion below. Rewrite the opinion to show that you feel strongly about what you are saying.

1. Older children teach their younger brothers and sisters.

   _____

   _____

2. Brothers and sisters share secrets.

   _____

   _____

3. Big brothers and sisters can show younger children how to make good choices.

   _____

   _____

4. Older children can do extra chores to help their parents.

   _____

   _____

5. An older child can play with younger brothers and sisters.

   _____

   _____

Name _____

Revising Your Personal Narrative

Put a check mark beside the sentences that describe your personal narrative.

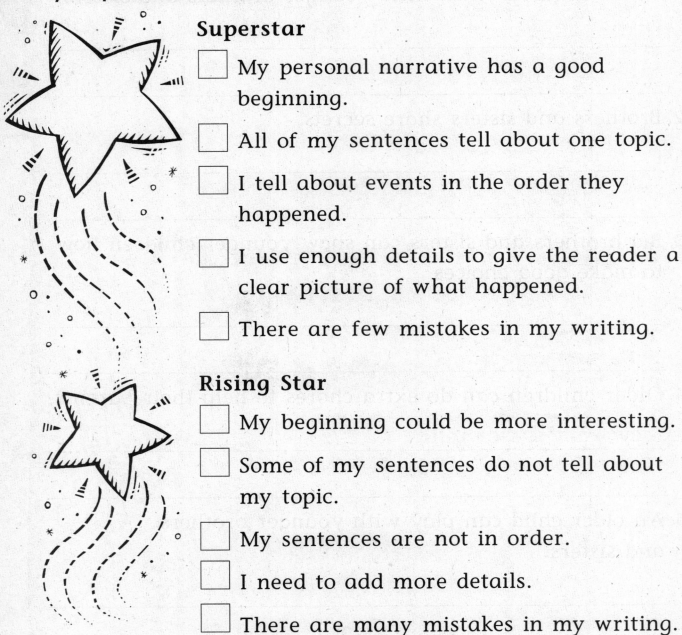

Superstar

☐ My personal narrative has a good beginning.

☐ All of my sentences tell about one topic.

☐ I tell about events in the order they happened.

☐ I use enough details to give the reader a clear picture of what happened.

☐ There are few mistakes in my writing.

Rising Star

☐ My beginning could be more interesting.

☐ Some of my sentences do not tell about my topic.

☐ My sentences are not in order.

☐ I need to add more details.

☐ There are many mistakes in my writing.

Name _____

Using Possessive Nouns

Read the sentences. Write the possessive form of the word in ( ).

1. This book <u>belongs to Dad.</u>

   This is _____ book. (Dad)

2. The pail <u>that belongs to Adam</u> is full of water.

   _____ pail is full of water. (Adam)

3. The feet <u>that belong to Mom</u> are sandy.

   _____ feet are sandy. (Mom)

4. The dog <u>that belongs to Adam</u> likes to run.

   _____ dog likes to run. (Adam)

5. They want to ride in the boat <u>that belongs to</u>
   <u>the girl.</u>

   They want to ride in the _____
   boat. (girl)

6. They went home in the car <u>that belongs to Bob.</u>

   They went home in _____ car. (Bob)

Name _____

Special Words for Writing

These Spelling Words are words that you use in your writing. Look carefully at how they are spelled.

Write the missing letters in the Spelling Words below. Use the words in the box to help you.

1. o___r

2. t___d___ ___

3. wou___d

4. a l___t

5. m___ny

6. w___r___

7. c_____ot

8. w___o

9. f___rst

10. h___r___

11. fr___ ___nd

12. c___ ___ld

Write the Spelling Words on the lines below.

_____ _____ _____

_____ _____ _____

_____ _____ _____

Name _____

Spelling Spree

Use Spelling Words to complete the sentences.

1. We are going to see dinosaurs

   _____ .

2. My _____ is coming too.

3. There will be _____ people
   at the museum.

4. Dad is driving _____ car.

5. Mom says, "We are _____ ."

6. We were _____ in line.

7. We _____ see the dinosaurs
   from far away.

8. The museum guide tells us _____
   about the dinosaurs.

9. Which Spelling Word is a compound

   word? _____

10. Which Spelling Word rhymes with **hood**?

    _____

Spelling Words

1. who
2. many
3. a lot
4. our
5. cannot
6. here
7. were
8. friend
9. first
10. would
11. today
12. could

Name _____

Proofreading and Writing

Proofreading Find and circle misspelled Spelling Words in this story. Then write each word correctly.

It was almost time for my party. Whoo would come first? My baby brother, Jamal, was sleeping. My aunts, uncles, and cousins wer coming soon. Meny people would be in our house today. My frend Juanita was the first to arrive. We cud not wait for the party to begin.

1. _____   4. _____

2. _____   5. _____

3. _____

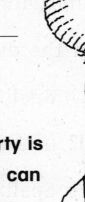

Write a Party Plan Plan a party. Tell who the party is for, when it will be, who will come, and games you can play. Write your ideas in sentences. Use as many Spelling Words as you can.

Name _____

Contractions

A contraction is a short way of writing one or more words.

Example: we + are = we're

Draw lines to match the contraction with the two words that make the contraction.

1. I'll   is not

2. isn't   could not

3. what's   I will

4. you're   what is

5. couldn't   you are

Write the word or words that make up each contraction.

6. I'm   _____

7. can't   _____

8. it's   _____

9. they're _____

10. we'll   _____

Name _____

Choosing -*le* Words

Read each sentence. Write the correct word in the blank.

1. We saw a duck _____
   across the path.

   | waddle battle |

2. The children started to _____
   when they heard the joke.

   | beetle giggle |

3. Carla ate a juicy red _____
   at lunch.

   | gurgle apple |

4. Now the baby is _____
   to walk.

   | able cuddle |

5. The stars _____ in the
   night sky.

   | twinkle rumble |

6. Jacob read a _____
   at school.

   | turtle fable |

7. Put three plates on the _____
   for breakfast.

   | bundle table |

8. The baby is asleep in the _____.

   | cradle marble |

Name _____

Discovering Vocabulary

Write the word from the box that goes with each clue.

Word Bank

| early | hair | instead |

1. means the opposite of late _____

2. something that grows on your head _____

3. rhymes with ahead _____

4. rhymes with curly _____

5. means "rather than" _____

6. rhymes with bear _____

7. a word that has one syllable or beat _____

Use each word from the box in a sentence.

8. _____

9. _____

10. _____

Name _____

Making Connections

Select a word from the box to complete each group of words.

```
                    Vocabulary

   bakery          cultures          customers
   dough           ingredients       recipes
```

1. _____ shoppers _____ buyers _____

2. _____ eggs _____ sugar _____

3. _____ brown bread _____ meatloaf _____

4. _____ shoe store _____ flower shop ___

Unscramble the vocabulary words.

5. utrlusce = _____

6. odhug = _____

Name _____

Following a Recipe Chart

As you read the story, write the steps you would follow to make each recipe.

(page 160) Steps to Make Pan Dulce	1. _____ 2. _____ 3. _____
(page 163) Steps to Make Pumpkin Turnovers	1. _____ 2. _____ 3. _____ 4. _____
(pages 166, 169) Steps to Make Bagels	1. _____ 2. _____ 3. _____ 4. _____ 5. _____ 6. _____ 7. _____

Name _____

Baking Story Ideas

1. Pablo helps make chango bars by

   _____ .

2. When Papa makes bagels he uses a family recipe

   that belonged _____ .

3. Three recipes that most likely come from

   Mamá's Mexican culture are _____

   _____ .

4. The treat that Pablo decides to take to

   International Day is _____

   _____ .

Name _____

Dog Fruit Salad

Read the recipe to learn how to make Dog Fruit Salad.

For each dog, you will need:

a pear cut in half

1 orange segment

1 prune

half of a cherry

1 raisin

1 plate

Directions:

1. Place the half pear on the plate.
2. Place the orange segment under the pear.
   This will be the dog's neck.
3. Put the prune on the wide end of the pear.
   This will be the dog's ear.
4. Put the half cherry at the narrow end of the pear.
   The cherry is the dog's nose.
5. To make the dog's eye, place the raisin between
   the ear and the nose.

This recipe makes one serving.

Name _____

Dog Fruit Salad continued

Use the recipe on page 97 to complete the chart below.

What I'll Make:

_____

What I'll Need:

_____

_____

_____

What I'll Do:

_____

_____

_____

_____

_____

_____

Name _____

Compare the Clues

Read each clue. Think about how the words are related.
Use a word from the box to complete each comparison.

Word Bank

ladder	paper	flower	whisper
butter	dancer	sister	spider

1. **Chalk** is to **chalkboard** as **pencil** is to _____.

2. **Loud** is to **soft** as **shout** is to _____.

3. **Ice** is to **skater** as **floor** is to _____.

4. **Boy** is to **girl** as **brother** is to _____.

5. **Nest** is to **bird** as **web** is to _____.

6. **Icing** is to **cake** as _____ is to **bread**.

7. **Walk** is to **path** as **climb** is to _____.

8. **Trunk** is to **tree** as **stem** is to _____.

Name _____

Charting Contractions

Each Spelling Word is a contraction. A contraction is a short way to write two words. An apostrophe takes the place of the letter or letters that are left out.

Circle the contraction that shows a short way to write *they + are*.

you'll   they're   I'm

Use Spelling Words to complete the chart below.

contractions using
will

1. _____

2. _____

3. _____

contractions using
is, are, or **am**

4. _____

5. _____

6. _____

contractions using
not

7. _____

8. _____

9. _____

contractions using
have

10. _____

11. _____

Name _____

Spelling Spree

Missing Letters Write the Spelling Word that is a contraction for each word or pair of words. Circle the letter or letters that the apostrophe takes the place of.

1. cannot _____

2. did not _____

3. is not _____

4. we have _____

5. I am _____

6. we will _____

7. you will _____

8. I have _____

1. I'll
2. we've
3. I'm
4. you're
5. isn't
6. didn't
7. you'll
8. I've
9. it's
10. we'll
11. can't *

they're

they   are

Name _____

Proofreading and Writing

Proofreading Kayla wrote the beginning of her report to the class about her group's project. Find and circle four Spelling Words that are spelled wrong. Then write each word correctly.

> I'm going to tell you about our group project. Is't been fun working together. Y'oure going to hear what we've learned about the culture we studied. We cannt tell you everything about this culture. There isn't enough time. But we'll share some interesting facts with you. I've got some pictures to show you. Il'l pass them around so everyone can see them.

1. _____ 3. _____

2. _____ 4. _____

Write a Report Write the beginning of a report you could give to your class. Use Spelling Words from the list. Write the beginning of your report on a separate sheet of paper.

Name _____

Double Meaning

Read the words and their definitions. Decide which meaning fits each sentence below. Write the correct definition.

check
  1. a mark to show something is correct
  2. to look for something

chip
  1. a small piece of something, such as chocolate
  2. to chop off a small piece

figure
  1. to solve
  2. a form, shape, or pattern

1. Nathan likes the **figure** in this picture.

_____

2. Can you **figure** out how to open this box?

_____

3. Darren counted to see how many chocolate **chips** were in his cookie.

_____

4. Patty can't find her math book. She will **check** to see if it is in her backpack.

_____

Now Verbs

▶ A verb is an action word. Verbs that tell about
now are action words that tell about things that
are happening now.

▶ An **s** is added to most verbs that tell about one person.

    Example: The boys **bake** bread.   The boy **bakes** bread.

Read the sentences. Write the verbs that tell about now.

1. The class reads the recipe. _____

2. Pedro slices the carrots for the salad. _____

3. Three children stir the cookie batter. _____

4. The children wait at the bus stop. _____

5. The family wants meat loaf for dinner. _____

6. We shop for food. _____

Name _____

Tell Me Now

Circle YES or NO to tell whether the verb is an action word that happens now.

1. bring   YES   NO

2. suggests   YES   NO

3. woke   YES   NO

4. runs   YES   NO

5. told   YES   NO

6. helped   YES   NO

Write each sentence so it tells about an action that happens now.

7. Tamara's mother poured sugar into the bowl.

_____

8. The fresh loaves of bread tasted good.

_____

9. Allen worked as a cook.

_____

10. The boys and girls made cookies.

_____

Now or Later?

**Rewrite the paragraph using verbs that tell
about things that are happening now.**

> Cathy got some oats, coconut, soybeans,
> sunflower seeds, and pieces of fruit. Cathy and
> her dad poured these into a bowl. Then Cathy's
> dad opened a bottle of oil. He twisted the top off
> a honey jar. They added the oil and honey to the
> mixture. Cathy's dad stirred the mixture. Next
> Cathy sprinkled the mixture on a flat pan. Finally
> Cathy's dad pushed the pan into the oven.

_____

_____

_____

_____

_____

_____

Name _____

Prompts for Writing

Follow the directions in each box.

Place a ✔ in front of the prompt you want to write about.

_____explanation   _____advertisement   _____compare and
                                                contrast

_____directions   _____story   _____description

Now write the word or words that are clues to the prompt you are going to write about.

_____

_____

Think about the prompt you have chosen and tell what you will write about.

_____

_____

List 3 details that you will include in your writing.

_____

_____

Name _____

Stick to the Point

Read through each paragraph. Then draw a line through the sentence that does not belong.

Earth Day is celebrated in April. Sometimes it is hot in April. People honor Earth on this special day. They help clean up their neighborhoods.

The Chinese New Year comes between January 21st and February 20th. On this day, families make special foods and put up colorful decorations. As part of the celebration, firecrackers are set off at midnight. Once I stayed up past midnight.

Yesterday my mother bought me a funny book of poems. A haiku is a short poem. It is usually about nature. This kind of poetry was first written in Japan.

Many African Americans celebrate Kwanzaa. The sun sets behind the hill. This holiday teaches about the African American culture. Kwanzaa teaches seven rules to live by.

A Native American powwow is like a huge party. The people wear special clothes. They celebrate by dancing, singing, eating, and telling stories. I like to dance.

Make New Words

Word Bank

frost   cream   luck   thirst

**Write the words in the box on the lines below. Next,
add *y* to the end of each word. Then use the new words
to finish the sentences.**

_____   _____

_____   _____

1. Yesterday I needed something to drink. I was

   so hot and _____.

2. I wanted something that was big, cold, and

   _____.

3. My mom mixed ice cream and bananas to

   make a _____ drink.

4. I'm _____ because my
   mom makes me special treats.

**On another sheet of paper write two sentences. Use
each word below in one of your sentences.**

snowy   stormy

Name _____

Un- Matches

Read each of the words in the box. Then read each of the meanings below. On the line beside each meaning, write the word from the box with the same meaning.

Word Bank

unlike	uncooked	unable	uneven
unreal	unbroken	unwell	untrue

1. can't do something _____

2. pretend _____

3. not smooth or straight _____

4. different _____

5. false _____

6. whole _____

7. raw _____

8. sick _____

unhappy

Name _____

Finish Up

**Finish each sentence with a word from the box.
You will need to use each word more than once.**

Word Bank

aunt   million   pair

1. My father's sister is my _____.

2. My _____ came over to help me
   get ready for my birthday party.

3. She says that the two of us are a great
   _____ of workers.

4. Before we get started, she puts on a
   comfortable _____ of shoes.

5. Then she hands me a _____ of
   scissors and tells me to cut strings for the balloons.

6. I tell her I'm going to cut a _____
   balloon strings.

7. She asks if I think I could count to a _____.

8. I say "Yes," and that I would like to have a
   _____ birthday parties!

Theme 5: **Family Time**   111

Name _____

Words for Bad Days

Use the words in the box to finish the story.

Vocabulary

angry   groaned   grumpily

fussed   grumbled   promised

Joey was having a bad day. He woke up

feeling _____. He had

_____ to help his dad in the

garden. He complained and _____

all day. He talked _____ to his

sister. When his brother asked him to play checkers,

he _____ about never winning.

Finally his dad came home from work. Joey

_____ and moaned some more.
Then he decided to help his dad plant tomatoes.
As they worked, Joey thought about how good
those tomatoes would taste. For the first time that
day, he smiled.

Name _____

What Do I Think? Chart

As you read, use the chart to keep track of how Alex behaves in the story. Think about how you might have felt if the same thing had happened to you.

What Alex Does	Why Alex Acts This Way
When Alex gets her hair braided, she does not hold still.	
Alex opens her first three gifts and complains about them.	
After Mother scolds Alex, Alex hugs and thanks her aunts.	
Alex opens her last gift and complains angrily.	
Alex breaks the carousel and then thinks about fixing it.	
When Alex's dad comes home, she greets him and says she is sorry about the carousel.	**What Do I Think About Alex?**

Name _____

Birthday Blues

**Finish each sentence so that it tells what
happened in *Carousel*.**

1. Alex was unhappy at her birthday party because

_____

2. Alex's mother sent her to bed because

_____

3. Alex whispered, "I'm sorry" to the zebra because

_____

4. Alex's father missed the party because

_____

5. Her father couldn't stay angry about not
   getting home on time because

_____

6. When Alex's mother winked at Alex and said,

   "It got a bit windy in here last night," she

_____

Making Judgments

Read the story. Then complete the chart on page 116.

Mike's Bad Day

When Mike got home from school, his Aunt
Bea was there.

"Look how much he has grown!" Aunt Bea
said. "And how handsome he is!" Mike didn't
like people to pay so much attention to him.

"Well, Mike, what do you say?" his mother
scolded him.

"Nothing," Mike said in a grumpy voice.

Aunt Bea tried to give him a big hug, but
Mike just stood there with his arms at his sides.

Mike's mother said, "Let's go for a walk."

"I don't want to," said Mike. "I have to do
my homework. Then I'm going to play with
Pepe." Pepe was Mike's best friend.

"But Aunt Bea came a long way to see you,"
said his mother.

Mike liked his aunt, but he wanted to play.

"No she didn't," said Mike. "She came to
see you. All you'll do is talk grown-up talk."
Then Mike went to his room and shut the door.
He could hear his mother and aunt talking
and laughing. He suddenly felt all alone.

Name _____

Making Judgments continued

After you've read the story about Mike, finish the chart.

What Happens in the Story?	What Happens in Response?	Why Does It Happen?
Aunt Bea talks about Mike.		
Aunt Bea tries to hug Mike.		
Mike's mother suggests a walk.		

What do you think about Mike's actions? Tell why.	

Name _____

Silly Pairs

Use a pair of words from the box to finish each silly sentence.

> puddle beetle   giggle battle   simple riddle
>
> little bottle   noodle doodle

1. An easy puzzle is a

   _____.

2. A laughing fight is a

   _____.

3. Silly writing with macaroni is a

   _____.

4. A bug in a little pond is a

   _____.

5. A jar that is too small to use is

   a _____.

Puppy Words

The words **puppy** and **baby** have two
syllables. The long **e** sound at the end of a
two-syllable word may be spelled **y**.

► The Spelling Word **cookie** does not
follow this pattern.

**Write the Spelling Words that end with the long *e*
sound spelled *y*.**

1. puppy
2. baby
3. lucky
4. happy
5. very
6. lady
7. funny
8. silly
9. many
10. only
11. cookie*

_____   _____

_____   _____

_____   _____

_____   _____

_____

**Write the Spelling Word
that ends with the
long *e* sound that is not
spelled with a *y*.**

_____

**On another sheet of paper, write a silly or funny story.
Use four of your Spelling Words in your story.**

Name _____

Spelling Spree

Rhyming Clues **Write a Spelling Word for each pair of clues.**

1. It rhymes with bunny. _____

2. It rhymes with penny. _____

3. It rhymes with hilly. _____

4. It rhymes with maybe. _____

5. It rhymes with guppy. _____

Spelling Words

1. puppy
2. baby
3. lucky
4. happy
5. very
6. lady
7. funny
8. silly
9. many
10. only
11. cookie*

Letter Math **Change the words below to Spelling Words. When you see the (−) sign, take away a letter. When you see the (+) sign, add a letter. Write the Spelling Word on the line.**

6. cooked − ed + ie = _____

7. vest − st + ry = _____

8. once − ce + ly = _____

9. land − n + y = _____

10. harp − r + py = _____

Name _____

Proofreading and Writing

Proofreading Circle four Spelling Words that are spelled wrong in the ad below. Then write each word correctly.

Bert's Pets

Make your son or daughter very

hapy today!

A kitten or pupy is the perfect

birthday gift.

We have manny pets to choose from.

Make today your child's luckee day!

1. puppy
2. baby
3. lucky
4. happy
5. very
6. lady
7. funny
8. silly
9. many
10. only
11. cookie*

1. _____   3. _____

2. _____   4. _____

 Write an Ad On a separate sheet of paper, write your own ad. Make it fun to read. Use Spelling Words from the list.

Keep Them Straight!

**Homophones are words that sound the same
but have different meanings and spellings.
Choose the correct homophone from the box
to complete each sentence.**

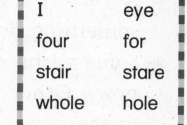

I	eye
four	for
stair	stare
whole	hole

1. The party was going to start at

   _____ o'clock.

   Davey couldn't wait _____ it to start.

2. He sat on a top _____ so he could
   see the people arrive.

   From there he could _____ at the big
   present his uncle brought.

3. His mother said, " _____ can't believe
   you are hiding up there!"

   Davey said, "I'm keeping an _____ on
   who comes in."

4. Davey's _____ family came to
   the party.
   The big candle they put on the cake made a

   _____ in the frosting.

Name _____

Past or Present?

▶ A verb is a word that tells what someone or
something does or is.

▶ Some verbs name actions that are happening
now. Other verbs name actions that happened
in the past.

▶ The letters **ed** are added to many verbs to
show that something happened in the past.

**Read each sentence. Circle the verb. If the verb tells
about something that happened in the past, put a ✔
on the line.**

1. _____ Alex liked all of her presents.

2. _____ She tells her friends about the pretty

carousel.

3. _____ She wanted her father to be at the

party.

4. _____ She watched the carousel in the dark.

5. _____ The carousel sits on the corner of her

desk.

6. _____ Alex followed the animals outside.

Name _____

Make a Choice

**Choose the best verb to finish each sentence.
Write it on the line.**

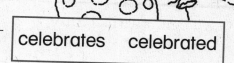

1. Last week Angie _____
   her birthday.

   | celebrates | celebrated |

2. Now she thinks she _____
   much older.

   | looks | looked |

3. At the party, Angie _____
   many presents.

   | opens | opened |

4. She and her friends _____
   lots of fun games.

   | plays | played |

5. They _____ party treats.

   | shares | shared |

6. When her baby brother popped a

   balloon, Angie _____ .

   | smiles | smiled |

7. After the party was over, Angie

   _____ her mother.

   | thanks | thanked |

8. She _____ she
   will have another party today!

   | hopes | hoped |

Make the Writing Better

**Read the card Maria has written. Circle the verbs that
are not correct. Then write them correctly.**

Dear Aunt Ruby,

    Thank you for the sweater you sent me for my

birthday. I am wearing it right now. It looked great with

the pants I am wearing.

    I'm sorry you miss the party yesterday. The day

before the party, Mom bakes a perfect cake. We all

cheer when she carried it into the dining room. Then

Mom and Aunt Julia serves the cake to everyone.

Yesterday was a great day. Just thinking about it

makes me wanted to have another piece of cake!

Your niece,

Maria

1. _____ 4. _____

2. _____ 5. _____

3. _____ 6. _____

Name _____

Get It Together!

Use the web below to gather information for your
paragraph. In the middle circle, write the subject of
your paragraph. As you gather information about the
subject, write it in the other circles. Then use this web
to help you write your paragraph.

Write one sentence that tells what your paragraph is about.

_____

Name _____

Information, Please

Read the information paragraph about emus. Look for ways to combine sentences. Then rewrite the paragraph by combining some of the sentences.

Emus are birds. They are large birds. Emus live mostly in Australia. They have long necks. They have long legs. They can be up to six feet tall. They can weigh up to 75 pounds. Emus can run as fast as 40 miles an hour. Their legs are strong. They can break a fence with one kick. Emus have wings. Emus can't fly. Emus are amazing birds.

_____

_____

_____

_____

_____

_____

Thunder Cake

Phonics Skill Base Words
and Endings *-ed, -ing*
(double final consonant)

Adding Endings

Write the base word and ending for each underlined word.

1. The rain was <u>beginning</u> to fall fast.

   _____   _____

   base word   ending

2. The girl <u>stepped</u> around the puddles.

   _____   _____

   base word   ending

3. She was <u>getting</u> very wet.

   _____   _____

   base word   ending

4. Lightning <u>ripped</u> across the sky.

   _____   _____

   base word   ending

5. She heard thunder <u>clapping</u> loudly.

   _____   _____

   base word   ending

6. Finally she started <u>running</u>.

   _____   _____

   base word   ending

Name _____

Word Search

Find and circle six words with the silent consonants in *gh*,

***kn*, or *b*. Write the words on the lines below.**

```
j   y   c   f   k   n   e   e
k   l   a   m   b   b   e   f
t   a   u   g   h   t   n   o
l   r   g   k   n   o   c   k
s   l   h   t   k   n   w   o
m   i   t   x   l   i   m   b
```

1. _____

2. _____

3. _____

4. _____

5. _____

6. _____

Name _____

Rhyming Fun

Finish each rhyme with a word from the box.

Word Bank

air   child   heavy   hour

Thunder and lightning? We don't care!

The smell of Thunder Cake is in the _____.

Mix the egg, then add the flour.

We'll eat Thunder Cake in just one _____!

Grandma's Thunder Cake is baked just right.

It's not _____ ; it's sweet and light.

"Come here, _____, and have a taste.

Don't let this Thunder Cake go to waste!"

Name _____

Weather Report

Follow these directions to draw a picture inside the frame.

1. Draw a line for the horizon.
2. Draw storm clouds in the sky.
3. Draw a bolt of lightning coming from the clouds.

Vocabulary

bolt
horizon
lightning
rumbled
thunder
weather

Use words from the box to help you answer these questions.

4. What is the weather like in your drawing?

_____

5. Think about the last time there was a storm. What sound did you hear after you saw lightning?

_____

Sequence of Events Chart

Complete this chart as you read *Thunder Cake*.

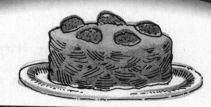

Beginning Pages 226–233

In the House

Grandma decides to bake a _____. She

teaches her grandchild to start counting when she sees

_____ and to stop when she _____ .

Middle Pages 234–243

On the Farm

Grandma and grandchild collect fresh _____ from

mean old _____ , fresh _____

from mean old _____ , a sack of _____

from the dark and scary _____ , and three

_____ from high up on the _____ .

End Pages 244–253

Back in the Warm Kitchen

Grandma and her grandchild _____

_____ .

Name _____

Letter Home

Here is a letter the girl in *Thunder Cake* might have written. Fill in the missing parts of her letter.

Dear Mama,

    Yesterday was a special day. It began to thunder, and I

was so scared that I _____.

Grandma told me we had to _____.

She taught me how to tell _____.

First you see the lightning. Then you _____

_____.

    We got eggs and _____ from the barn. Then

we got chocolate, sugar, and flour from the _____.

Last we got tomatoes and _____. Then we made

the cake.

    Grandma told me I was brave because I _____

_____. I really did feel brave!

               I miss you,

               Your daughter

Name _____

Follow the Events

Read the story below.

Fish Story

One sunny afternoon, Sam and his grandfather went fishing. They walked through the woods to the edge of the lake. Sam found a log for them to sit on. His grandfather set up their poles and put worms on the hooks. While they sat on the log fishing, Sam's grandfather told stories.

Soon Sam had a bite on his line. He reeled the line in and caught his first fish. Sam was so excited that he almost fell into the water. His grandfather helped him get the fish off the hook and put it in the bucket. Together they sat talking and fishing until big black clouds blocked the sun.

"Uh-oh, looks like a storm is coming," said Sam's grandfather. Just then thunder rumbled. Rain was falling across the lake.

"That rain will be here soon," said Sam's grandfather.

They packed their things. As they walked back through the woods, the rain began to pour down.

"This looks serious!" said Sam's grandfather.

When they got to the car, they were soaking wet. Sam was cold, but he was happy. He had caught ten fish!

Name _____

Follow the Events continued

Write the events from the box in the order in which they happened.

Thunder rumbles and rain falls.

Grandfather sets up the fishing poles.

Sam catches his first fish.

Sam and Grandfather walk through the woods to the lake.

They quickly pack their things and walk back to the car.

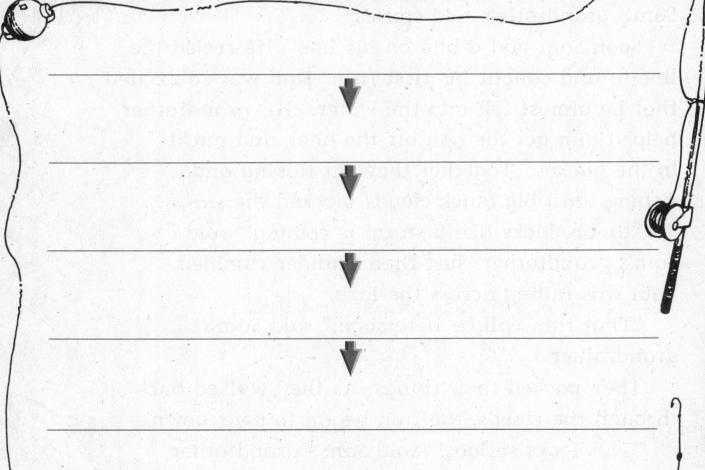

_____

_____

_____

_____

Name _____

Matching Rhymes

Write a word from the box that rhymes with each word in dark print.

Word Bank

sunny	plenty	thirty	bumpy	lobby	nifty

1. My grandmother owns **twenty** cake pans.

   _____

2. Baking is her **hobby**. _____

3. She can bake **fifty** kinds of cakes!

   _____

4. I help her wash the **dirty** dishes.

   _____

5. We tell **funny** jokes while we wash.

   _____

6. I can't be **grumpy** at my

   grandmother's farm.

   _____

Name _____

Word Sort

Some words end with a short vowel sound
followed by one consonant. The final
consonant in these words is usually doubled
before **-ed** or **-ing** is added.

Write the Spelling Words that end with *-ed*.

stopped

_____ _____

_____

1. batted
2. running
3. clapped
4. stopped
5. getting
6. shopping
7. stepped
8. hugging
9. pinned
10. sitting

Write the Spelling Words that end with *-ing*.

running

_____ _____

_____

**On a separate sheet of paper, write two sentences. In one
sentence use a Spelling Word that ends in *-ed*. In the
other sentence, use a Spelling Word that ends in *-ing*.**

Spelling Spree

Puzzle Play Write a Spelling Word for each clue.

1. cheered with hands

   _____ □ _____

2. what you are doing in a chair

   _____ □ _____

3. having something come to you

   □ _____

4. going to a store to buy things

   _____ □ _____

5. not moving _____ □ ,_____

6. held down _____ □ _____

1. batted
2. running
3. clapped
4. stopped
5. getting
6. shopping
7. stepped
8. hugging
9. pinned
10. sitting

Write the letters in boxes below. The letters will spell a word that names something you see in a storm.

_____ing

Letter Swap Make Spelling Words by using a doubled letter from the box in place of the letters in dark print. Write the words.

nn   tt   pp   gg

7. hu**mm**ing _____

8. ste**mm**ed _____

Proofreading and Writing

Proofreading **Circle four Spelling Words that are spelled wrong in this story. Then write each word correctly.**

Spelling Words

1. batted
2. running
3. clapped
4. stopped
5. getting
6. shopping
7. stepped
8. hugging
9. pinned
10. sitting

Anna and her grandmother played softball at the family picnic. It was the last inning. Anna bated first. She hit the ball hard. While she was runing to first base, her whole team claped. She was safe! Then her grandmother steped up to the plate. She hit a home run. Their team won! The players sitting on the bench began hugging each other. What a game!

1. _____   3. _____

2. _____   4. _____

Write a Story **Write a story about a girl or boy and a grandmother. Use Spelling Words from the list. Write your story on a separate sheet of paper.**

Name _____

Look It Up

Read each word. Can you find it in the dictionary? For some you will need to drop the ending and look up the base word. For each one, write the word you would find in the dictionary.

1. climbing _____

2. sting _____

3. knowing _____

4. chopped _____

5. thread _____

6. stepping _____

7. fanning _____

8. writing _____

9. next _____

10. clogged _____

Name _____

To Be or Not to Be

Some verbs tell about something that happens in the present. Other verbs tell about something that happened in the past.

► **Is** and **are** tell about something that happens in the present.

► **Was** and **were** tell about something that happened in the past.

Look at the picture. Answer the questions with a sentence using *is*, *are*, *was*, or *were*.

1. Where was the cake?

_____

2. Who is in the kitchen?

_____

3. How many places were set at the table?

_____

4. Who is waiting to eat?

_____

5. What is the girl holding?

_____

6. What are they going to do with the cake?

_____

Time Change

Change these sentences from present to past.

1. Grandma is in her chair.

_____

2. The girls are outside.

_____

3. The cat is in the window.

_____

Change these sentences from past to present.

4. The dogs were in the kitchen.

_____

5. The girls were playing near the barn.

_____

6. The cow was waiting to be milked.

_____

Name _____

Past and Present

Read the biography. Circle the verbs that are used incorrectly. Write the correct verbs below.

My grandmother are an amazing person. She is a nurse when she was young. She were working in a hospital in India. There is many patients there who liked her. Some of them still write to her today. I think they was lucky to meet her!

1. _____

2. _____

3. _____

4. _____

5. _____

Name _____

Who's Speaking?

Use this chart to help you describe the speakers you will include in your writing.

	Speaker 1	Speaker 2
Who is the speaker?		
Write 3 words to describe the speaker.		
What does the speaker want?		
How does the speaker talk? (Circle one.)	Long sentences and big words Funny Many describing words	Long sentences and big words Funny Many describing words

Name _____

Improve the Writing

Read the dialogue. Then rewrite it below, correcting capitals and punctuation that are incorrect.

"Grandma, what were you like when you were a girl? asked Mina.

Oh, about like you, I suppose," she said.

"what do you mean" asked Mina.

Grandma looked very serious. "I liked cake better than carrots. I liked to climb trees. And I asked too many questions.

Mina and her grandma laughed, and their laughs sounded just the same.

_____

_____

_____

_____

_____

_____

_____

Name _____

Writing an Answer to a Question

Use what you have learned about taking tests to help you write answers to questions about something you have read. This practice will help you when you take this kind of test.

Read these paragraphs from the selection *Brothers and Sisters*.

>Sometimes it's hard to be a younger brother.
>
>"It's not fair!" says Peter. "Just because she's older, my sister can do everything better."
>
>And sometimes it's great to be a younger brother.
>
>"She's my other mom," says Steven.

Name _____

Writing an Answer to a Question continued

Now write your answer to each question.

1. From these paragraphs, what can you tell about being a younger brother?

_____

_____

_____

_____

2. Why do you think an older sister is usually better at doing things than a younger brother?

_____

_____

_____

_____

Name _____

Spelling Review

Write Spelling Words from the list to answer the questions.

1–9. Which words end with **er**, **ed**, or **ing**?

1. _____   6. _____

2. _____   7. _____

3. _____   8. _____

4. _____   9. _____

5. _____

10–15. Which words are contractions?

10. _____   13. _____

11. _____   14. _____

12. _____   15. _____

16–20. Which words end with the long **e** sound?

16. _____   19. _____

17. _____   20. _____

18. _____

Spelling Words

1. isn't
2. hugging
3. silly
4. getting
5. sister
6. it's
7. clapped
8. mother
9. I'm
10. happy
11. lady
12. better
13. I've
14. puppy
15. sitting
16. brother
17. I'll
18. baby
19. you're
20. stopped

Name _____

Spelling Spree

Puzzle Play **Write a Spelling Word for each clue.**
Use the letters in boxes to spell a family feeling.

Spelling Words

1. struck hands together

   ___ ☐ ___ ___ ___ ___ ___

2. the opposite of **sister**

   ___ ___ ☐ ___ ___ ___ ___

3. contraction made by leaving out the

   letters **ha** ___ ' ☐ ___

4. ended ___ ___ ___ ___ ___ ☐ ___

Secret Word: ___ ___ ___ ___ ___

Write a Spelling Word to finish each sentence.

5. "Are you _____ a cold?"

6. "The _____ next door gave us some soup."

7. "The _____ doesn't like this dog food!"

8. "Dad's cold is _____ today."

9. "Put the _____ in her crib."

10. "No, it _____ my day to do the dishes!"

Spelling Words

1. brother
2. isn't
3. stopped
4. getting
5. I've
6. lady
7. better
8. baby
9. puppy
10. clapped

Name _____

Proofreading and Writing

Proofreading Circle four Spelling Words that are wrong. Then write each one correctly.

> I hope your'e coming to my house later to play. Im now the owner of a really cute kitten. He likes to act sillie. I think you'll like huging him.

1. sister
2. sitting
3. mother
4. I'll
5. you're
6. I'm
7. happy
8. silly
9. hugging
10. it's

1. _____ 3. _____

2. _____ 4. _____

Take a Look! Write Spelling Words to finish this story.

My _____ and my _____

5.
6.

love to bake. Tanya is _____ on the chair.

7.

She looks _____ . Someday, _____

8.
9.

help too. I think _____ fun to eat what they make!

10.

Write a Poem On another sheet of paper, write a poem.
Use the Spelling Review Words.

Name _____

We Are All the Same

Fill in each section below.

Ellen Ochoa, Theodore Roosevelt, and Wilma Rudolph are similar in many ways. I think this way is the most important.

_____

_____

_____

Here are some of the ways I am like Ellen Ochoa, Theodore Roosevelt, and Wilma Rudolph.

This is How I Am Like Ellen Ochoa	This is How I Am Like Theodore Roosevelt	This is How I Am Like Wilma Rudolph

Name _____

Key Events

Fill in the chart with what you think are the most important events in each category.

	Ellen Ochoa	Theodore Roosevelt	Wilma Rudolph
What happened in their childhood?			
What school subjects did they work hard at?			
What did they do when they grew up?			

Name _____

Talent Show

Plan a classroom or school-wide Talent Fair. Use these questions to help you write your invitations.

Where will your Talent Fair take place?

_____

What time will it be?

_____

What day will it be held?

_____

Describe some of the activities that will take place there.

_____

_____

_____

_____

_____

Name _____

Talent Show

Fill in the chart as you read the stories.

	What types of talents did you read about in this theme?	How did talent and hard work help some of the characters in this theme?
The Art Lesson		
Moses Goes to a Concert		
The School Mural		

Name _____

Talented Words

Write the word from the box that completes each sentence.

Word Bank

| threw | clues | flew | moon | soup |

1. Carla knows all about the stars and

   _____. Someday, she might be an
   .

2. Sal likes to follow _____ to solve

   a mystery. Sal thinks he would like to be a
   .

3. Keisha likes to make _____.

   She wants to be a _____.

4. Yesterday, Sam _____ the ball really far.

   He thinks he would like to be a
   .

5. When Amy went on vacation she _____

   on a plane. Now she is sure she wants to be a
   .

Name _____

Words with Meaning

Write each word from the box after its meaning.

Word Bank

woman	fair	gold

1. A color that looks like bright yellow metal.

   _____

2. A grown-up girl. _____

3. To treat everyone the same. _____

**Use the words in the box to complete the sentences.
Then answer the questions.**

Pat and Judy entered a painting contest. Pat's

painting was selected as the winner. A _____

from the art gallery gave Pat a _____

medal. Both Pat and Judy worked hard on their

paintings. Do you think it is _____ that

only one girl received a gold medal? Tell why or

why not on the line below.

_____

Name _____

Picture This

Vocabulary

practice   ruin   smock   copy   powders   chalk   crayons

Use the words in the box to complete the sentences below.

Mickey, the Painter

Mickey loves to draw pictures. He uses

different kinds of art materials. Sometimes he uses

_____ and sometimes he uses

_____. Mostly he uses paint

_____ mixed with water. Mickey

finds time to _____ drawing

every day. He used to _____

pictures that other people had made. Now he

draws his own pictures. He always wears a

_____ when he paints. He

doesn't want to _____ his

clothes by getting paint on them.

Name _____

What the Author Thinks Chart

What the Author Says	What the Author Probably Thinks
Page 293: Tommy drew _____ everywhere he went. **Page 299**: Tommy drew pictures on his _____ .	What does the author think about drawing? _____ _____
Page 302: In kindergarten, the _____ didn't stick to the paper. **Page 303**: In the wind, the paint blew off the _____ .	What does the author think about painting in kindergarten? _____ _____
Page 313: Tommy wanted to use his own sixty-four _____ . **Page 313**: Tommy told the art teacher, "Real artists don't _____ ."	What does the author think about real artists? _____ _____

Name _____

Story Frame

Complete the story frame.

Tommy loved to _____ pictures.

He wanted to be an _____ when he

grew up. His twin cousins told him not to copy and

to _____ drawing pictures. Tommy

wanted to take art _____ at school.

He had to wait until _____ grade.

When the art teacher came, the children had to use

school crayons, copy a picture, and draw on one

piece of _____. Tommy would not

draw. The teachers said that it would not be

_____ for Tommy to do something

different. Finally, his teachers agreed that after

Tommy made a Pilgrim picture, he could use his own

box of _____ and draw a second

picture on another sheet of paper.

Theme 6: **Talent Show**   159

Name _____

Author's Viewpoint

Read the story. Then answer the questions on page 161.

Lana and the Art Contest

I was working on a math problem when Mr. Albert, my teacher, walked back into the classroom. He was smiling. "Lana, I have some great news for you. Your painting of a sailboat won first prize in the school's art contest. We would like to frame your painting and hang it in the office."

I gasped with surprise. I had forgotten about the painting I turned in last month.

"The school wants to keep my painting?" I asked. "I would love that! Thank you for telling me such exciting news, Mr. Albert!"

The bell rang. I ran to my desk and shoved the books into my bag. I couldn't wait to tell my mom the news. I ran home so fast that I got an ache in my side.

As soon as I opened the door, I shouted. "Mom, where are you? I won! I won the school art contest! They want to hang my painting in the office."

Mom smiled and hugged me. "You are a very good artist," she said. "Your hours of practice have been worth the time. I am so proud of you."

Name _____

Author's Viewpoint continued

After you've read the story about Lana and the art contest, answer the questions below.

1. How does the author feel about winning the prize?

    _____

    _____

2. Write two words the author used to show these feelings.

    _____

    _____

3. Write two things the author did that show these feelings.

    _____

    _____

4. What else might the author have done to show her feelings?

    _____

    _____

Name _____

Action Words

Write the correct ending for each base word in dark print.

1. Mei Ling likes to **tap**.

She _____ in her dance

class yesterday. Today she is

_____ in a talent show.

2. Dan likes to **pot** plants.

He _____ two plants for

his mother.

Now he is _____ a plant

for his dad's office.

3. Beth Ann likes to **hug** her pets.

First she _____ her dog.

Now she is _____ her cat.

Name _____

Moon and Book

Most of the Spelling Words are spelled with
the letters **oo**. These letters make two
different sounds. They make the sounds
you hear in **moon** and **book**.

► The word **you** is special. The vowels **ou**
spell the same vowel sound that you hear
in **moon**.   The word w**ho** is special.
The vowel **o** spells the same vowel sound
that you hear in **moon**.

**Write each Spelling Word under the picture with
the same vowel sound.**

Spelling Words
1. zoo
2. tooth
3. hook
4. moon
5. book
6. soon
7. took
8. good
9. room
10. foot
11. you *
12. who *

_____   _____

_____   _____

_____   _____

_____   _____

Name _____

Spelling Spree

Write a Spelling Word to finish each sentence.

1. A doctor can take care of a hurt

   _____.

2. An astronaut knows all about the

   _____.

3. A librarian can help _____

   find a _____.

4. A dentist knows what to do about an

   aching _____.

5. A person _____ likes animals

   might work in a _____.

6. A carpenter can make a house bigger by

   adding a new _____.

Proofreading and Writing

Proofreading Circle the four Spelling Words that are misspelled in this story. Write each word correctly.

Dear Rachel,

You will not believe what happened today! I went to an art show. I tuk my painting of the moon. I hung it on a hock. Guess who was there? My teacher, Mrs. Watson, had come to look at the art show. She said my painting was very gud. She wanted to buy it. I was so happy. Sune I hope to be a famous painter.

Your friend,

Mike

Spelling Words

1. zoo
2. tooth
3. hook
4. moon
5. book
6. soon
7. took
8. good
9. room
10. foot
11. you *
12. who *

1. _____   3. _____

2. _____   4. _____

✏️ **Write About Yourself** What do you like to do? Do you have a special talent? Write about it on a separate piece of paper. Use Spelling Words from the list.

Name _____

Playing with Word Families

In each sentence, write a word from the word family _play_.

Word Bank

plays	played	playing	player	playful	playground

1. Marco is a baseball _____ .

2. Marco goes to the _____ to

   practice every day.

3. Yesterday, his friend _____ ball

   with him.

4. Sometimes Marco _____

   ball with his dog.

5. Marco is _____ ball

   with his dog today.

6. The _____ puppy

   just ran off with the ball.

Name _____

Show What's Been Done

Many verbs add **-ed** to show past action.
► Verbs that do not add **-ed** to show past action do not
  follow a pattern or rule for their spelling changes.

Mr. Jones made a list of things to do before the talent

show. He started another list to show what he had done.

Complete the second list to show that Mr. Jones got

everything done.

To Do List

  1. Pick up tickets from
     the office.

  2. Give the tickets to
     the teacher.

  3. Draw a poster to show
     the ticket price.

  4. Blow up balloons for
     the stage.

  5. Make blue paint.

Second List

   1. Picked up tickets from the office.

  2. _____

  _____

  3. _____

  _____

  4. _____

  _____

  5. _____

  _____

Name _____

Show the Past Without -ed

Many verbs add **-ed** to the end to show past
action, but some verbs do not follow this pattern.

► Verbs that do not add **-ed** to show past action
   do not follow a pattern or rule for their
   spelling changes.

Write the word that completes each sentence.

1. Allison and Josie are lucky, because

   they _____ an artist now.

know   knew

2. They _____ art lessons from
   her each week.

take   took

3. They _____ to their lessons
   every Tuesday.

go   went

4. Last week they _____
   pictures of flowers.

draw   drew

5. Another time they _____
   clay animals.

make   made

6. Next week, Allison and Josie

   _____ to try something new.

get   got

Name _____

Irregular Verbs

**When Olivia went to visit her grandmother, she wrote a
postcard to her friend. She made some mistakes. Find
and circle four verbs that are not written correctly.
Write them correctly.**

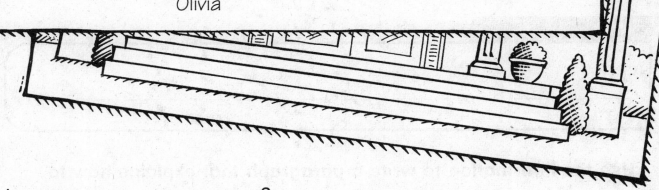

Dear Benjy,

　　Grandma and I are having so much fun! Last week,
Grandma take me to a big art museum. We rode the bus
downtown. I see some really big paintings. An artist was
there. He give me a box of crayons. He told me I could be an
artist someday, too. Now I drew all the time. When I come
home, I will show you my box of crayons. We can draw
pictures together.

　　　　　Your best friend,

　　　　　Olivia

1. _____   3. _____

2. _____   4. _____

Name _____

Getting Started

Look at the comic strip to find out how powder becomes paint. Write down the steps.

How to Mix Paint

First

_____

Next

_____

Now

_____

Use the information to write a paragraph that explains how to make paint from a powder mix. Write your paragraph on another sheet of paper.

Name _____

Complete the Sentence

Read the sentences and the sentence parts. Rewrite the parts so that they are complete sentences.

How Maria Makes a Clay Animal

1. First, Maria gets a lump of clay.
2. Shapes the clay into a ball.

_____

_____

3. Next she makes the animal's body.
4. Then the head and legs.

_____

_____

5. Uses little pieces of clay for ears and a tail.

_____

_____

6. Finally, the clay animal.

_____

_____

Name _____

Revising Your Instructions

Check the boxes next to the sentences that describe your draft.

Superstar

☐ I wrote an interesting topic sentence.

☐ Each step is clear and complete.

☐ I included all the steps and wrote them in order.

☐ I used time-order words, such as **first**, **next**, **then**, and **finally**.

☐ The ending makes the reader want to try my instructions.

☐ My instructions have only a few mistakes.

Rising Star

☐ I need a more interesting topic sentence.

☐ Some steps are missing or are out of order.

☐ Some steps are unclear or are not complete.

☐ I could add some time-order words.

☐ My instructions have many mistakes.

Name _____

How to Grow a Sunflower

Cross out the verb in each step. Write the exact verb that best completes each step.

Word Bank

| place | dig | shovel |

1. First, make a hole. _____

2. Next, get the seed in the hole.

   _____

3. Then, put dirt on the seed.

   _____

Write a sentence for a final step in growing a sunflower. Use an exact verb.

_____

_____

_____

_____

Name _____

Spelling Words

These Spelling Words are words that you use in your writing. Look carefully at how they are spelled.

Write the missing letters in the Spelling Words below. Use the words in the box to help you.

1. s t_____ted

2. tr_____d

3. o_____er

4. com_____

5. p_____ple

6. s_____met_____ing

7. s_____ool

8. outs_____e

9. go_____g

10. n_____w

11. v_____ry

12. n_____v_____r

Spelling Words

1. tried
2. never
3. going
4. outside
5. coming
6. new
7. very
8. school
9. other
10. started
11. something
12. people

Write the Spelling Words below.

_____   _____

_____   _____

_____   _____

_____   _____

Name _____

Spelling Spree

Write a Spelling word in the star for each clue.

1. a place to learn
2. to begin
3. moving away
4. not old
5. moving toward
6. persons

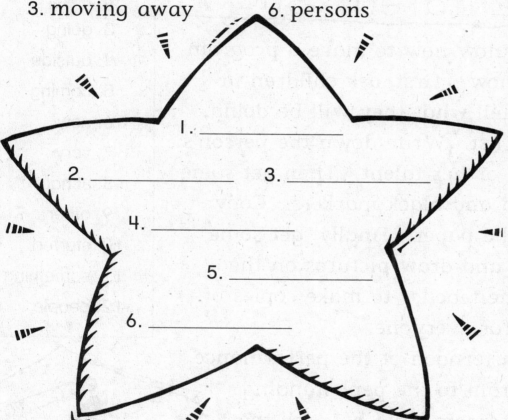

1. _____
2. _____
3. _____
4. _____
5. _____
6. _____

1. tried
2. never
3. going
4. outside
5. coming
6. new
7. very
8. school
9. other
10. started
11. something
12. people

Write a Spelling Word to complete each sentence.

7. We _____ to sing a song.

8. But _____ went wrong.

9. The piano player _____ came.

10. We were _____ sad.

Theme 6: **Talent Show**   175

Name _____

Proofreading and Writing

Proofreading Find and circle misspelled Spelling
Words below. Then write each word correctly.

1. tried
2. never
3. going
4. outside
5. coming
6. new
7. very
8. school
9. other
10. started
11. something
12. people

Grade 2 Talent Show

Do you know how to make a program
for a talent show? First, ask children in
your class to tell what they will be doing.
Next, make a list. Write down the person's
name and his or her talent. Then get some
paper and red and black markers. Copy
the list onto the paper. Finally, get some
otha markers and draw pictures on the
paper. Ask the teacher to make copies of
the program for everyone.

On the afternoon of the performance,
give the program to the pepl standing
outsid the classroom. We hope all the
parents are comeing. We have tryed our
best to put on a great show.

1. _____   4. _____

2. _____   5. _____

3. _____

Name _____

Sorting Long *i* Words

Write each word from the box under a word that rhymes and that spells the long *i* sound the same way.

Word Bank

bright	die	fright	lie
might	sigh	pie	tight

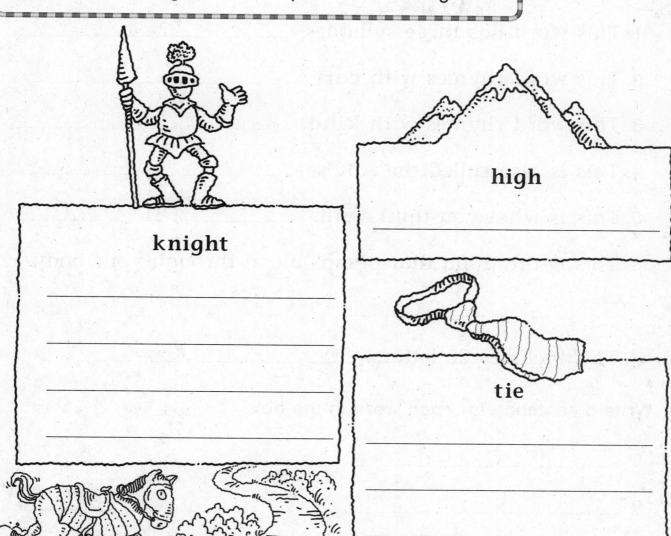

knight

_____

_____

_____

high

_____

tie

_____

_____

Name _____

Word Wizard

Write the word from the box that goes with each clue.

Word Bank

| heart | mind | alphabet |

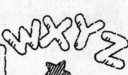

1. This word has three syllables. _____

2. This word rhymes with **cart**. _____

3. This word rhymes with **kind**. _____

4. This is also called the ABC's. _____

5. This is what you think with. _____

6. This is the thing that pumps blood through your body.

_____

7. This includes 26 letters. _____

Write a sentence for each word in the box.

8. _____

9. _____

10. _____

Name _____

Questions and Answers

Read what Nancy asked John about his deaf sister.
Finish John's answers using words from the box.

Word Bank

deaf	vibration	signs
percussion	instruments	hearing

Nancy: What kind of problem does your sister have?

John: My sister is _____ .

Nancy: What does that mean?

John: She has a problem with her

_____ .

Nancy: How do you talk to her?

John: She _____ words with her hands.

Nancy: If your sister can't hear, how can she enjoy music?

John: She feels the _____ from
the instruments.

Nancy: Which _____
does she like?

John: She told me she likes all the

_____ instruments.

Noting Details Chart

As you read the story, complete the chart below.

Find details to support each statement.

Details Chart
Moses can't hear the sounds he makes on the drum. (page 333)   _____   _____
Mr. Samuels's friend is a percussionist. (pages 342 and 344)   _____   _____
The percussionist and children feel the music at the concert. (pages 344–345)   _____   _____
The children meet the percussionist. (pages 352–355)   _____   _____

Name _____

Connecting Story Ideas

Put together the two pieces of each sentence to tell about the story. Write the complete sentences.

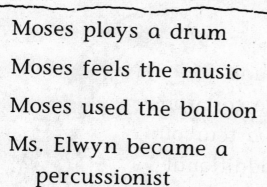

Moses plays a drum

Moses feels the music

Moses used the balloon

Ms. Elwyn became a percussionist

even though he's deaf.

by working hard.

through his hands and feet.

to feel the vibrations.

1. _____

_____

2. _____

_____

3. _____

_____

4. _____

_____

Name _____

Noting Details

Read the information below. Complete the chart on page 183.

The Dinosaur Museum

General Information

The museum is open Monday through Friday from 8 A.M. until 5 P.M. The cost for having a guide take your class on a tour of the museum is $50. If you need additional information, please call 555-1212.

Exhibits

Dinosaurs once roamed Earth. At the museum, you will see many different kinds of dinosaurs, including baby dinosaurs and dinosaur eggs. You will even see real dinosaur footprints made in stone!

Rules

We have a few important rules at the museum. Food and drinks should not be brought into the building. The class must stay with the guide so that students don't get lost in the museum. Please do not touch the exhibits since they can be damaged. Thank you for your cooperation.

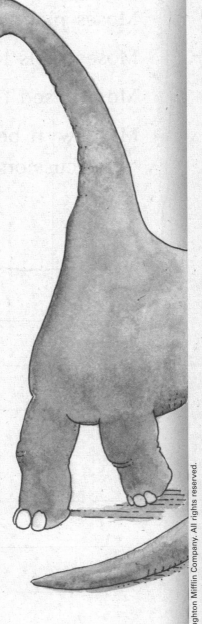

Name _____

Noting Details continued

After you've read the information on page 182, complete this chart. Give details about the Dinosaur Museum.

General Information	Exhibits	Rules
_____	_____	_____
_____	_____	_____
_____	_____	_____
_____	_____	_____
_____	_____	_____
_____	_____	_____
_____	_____	_____
_____	_____	_____
_____	_____	_____
_____	_____	_____
_____	_____	_____

Name _____

Cool Vowel Pairs

Read the silly sentences. Circle the words that have the vowel sound you hear in *soon*.

1. A boot flew over the moon.

2. Jill ate her blue soup.

3. Sam threw a tree into his room.

4. The group of birds sat on a new statue.

Now write each circled word under the word that spells the vowel sound the same way.

spoon

stew

_____

_____

_____

glue

group

_____

_____

Name _____

Long *i* Words

Each Spelling Word has the long i sound.
This vowel sound may be spelled i, **y**, or **igh**.
The words **eye** and **buy** also have the long i
sound, but they are spelled differently.

**Write each Spelling Word in the column with the
same long *i* spelling.**

long **i**
spelled **y**

_____

_____

_____

_____

long **i** sound
spelled **igh**

_____

_____

_____

long **i** sound
spelled **i**

_____

Spelling Words

1. sky
2. find
3. night
4. high
5. fly
6. try
7. light
8. dry
9. right
10. mind
11. eye*
12. buy*

**Write a Spelling Word to finish each sentence.
Choose a word that has a star next to it.**

1. I went to the store to _____ a kite.

2. Don't put a sharp pencil near your _____.

Name _____

Spelling Spree

Write a Spelling Word for each clue in the puzzle.

Across

1. I will _____ to do my best.

2. Did you _____ your lost pencil?

3. The stars shine at _____.

4. Mom wants me to _____ the dishes.

5. Do you _____ sharing your
   book with me?

7. I see better with my left _____.

Down

2. I wish I could _____ like a bird.

6. I will save money
   to _____ that new toy.

1. sky
2. find
3. night
4. high
5. fly
6. try
7. light
8. dry
9. right
10. mind
11. eye*
12. buy*

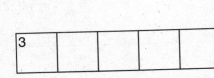

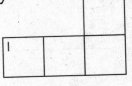

Name _____

Proofreading and Writing

Proofreading Find and circle four Spelling Words that are spelled wrong in the poem. Then write each word correctly.

If I Could Fly

I wish I could fly
Wherever I please,
Hygh up in the skye
And over tall trees.

Way up I would go
As lite as a bird,
Then swoop way down low
And never be heard.

I'd turn to the left
And turn to the rit.
I'd fly all day long
And into the night.

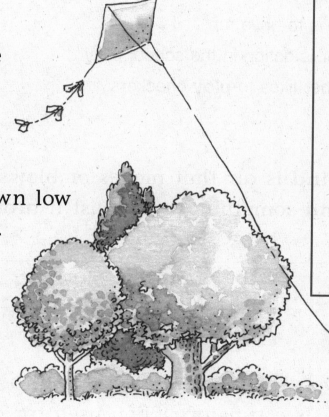

1. sky
2. find
3. night
4. high
5. fly
6. try
7. light
8. dry
9. right
10. mind
11. eye*
12. buy*

1. _____   3. _____

2. _____   4. _____

Write a Poem Write a poem using Spelling Words from the list. Write your poem on a separate piece of paper.

Name _____

What Do You Mean?

Read the different meanings for each word.
Then write a sentence for each meaning.

Example: **play**

A **play** is a kind of story that people act in.

To **play** is to have fun.

My sister is acting in the school **play**.

My brother likes to **play** checkers.

wind

The **wind** is air that moves or blows.

To **wind** something is to twist it around.

1. _____

2. _____

bow

A **bow** is the piece of wood used to play a violin.

A **bow** is a type of ribbon used for decoration.

To **bow** means to bend forward at the waist.

3. _____

4. _____

5. _____

188   Theme 6: **Talent Show**

Name _____

Colorful Adjectives

Color red all the puzzle pieces that have adjectives written on them.

An **adjective** tells about a noun. Some adjectives tell what kind or how many.

► The words **a**, **an**, and **the** do not do this. They are special adjectives.

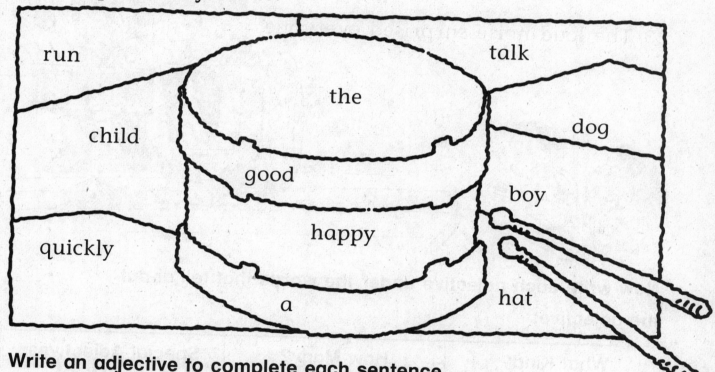

run   talk

child   dog

the

good

boy

quickly   happy

a   hat

Write an adjective to complete each sentence.

1. There are _____ musicians in the band.

2. _____ conductor is their leader.

3. The musicians play _____ music.

4. They play in a _____ concert hall.

Name _____

Hunting for Adjectives

Find and circle eight adjectives in the sentences below.

1. Three big drums sat on the quiet stage.

2. All of a sudden, Lisa started banging

   on two drums.

3. The loud noise surprised everyone.

Now write each adjective under the words that tell about

the adjective.

What Kind?	How Many?	Special Adjectives (a, an, the)
_____	_____	_____
_____	_____	_____
_____	_____	_____

Name _____

Practice with Adjectives

Rena wants her parents to let her take piano lessons. She made this list to convince them. Make each sentence on her list more interesting by adding adjectives.

1. I will learn how to play

_____ music.

2. I will practice _____ hours every day.

3. Lessons will only cost _____ dollars.

4. I can play _____ piano at concerts.

5. I will give a _____ concert each year.

Name _____

Planning a Summary

Plan a summary of a story you have read. Answer the questions below.

Who are the main characters?
_____

Where does the story take place?
_____

What is the problem in the story? (Look at the beginning of the story.)
_____

What happens when the characters try to solve the problem? (Look at the middle of the story.)
_____

How is the problem solved? (Look at the end of the story.)
_____

Name _____

Make It Short

Write a sentence that summarizes each paragraph below.

Kites have been around for a long time. They have also carried special instruments to learn more about weather. Some kites were even used to make signals during wars.

1. _____

_____

Porcupine fish get their name from their sharp spines. They are able to puff themselves up with air or water. They can make themselves twice as big as they usually are.

2. _____

_____

Here are some things that will help you do your best when you take a test. First, listen carefully to the directions before beginning. Second, read all questions and answers carefully. Third, take time to check your answers.

3. _____

_____

Name _____

Adding Endings

Add the -ed and -ing endings to each base word.

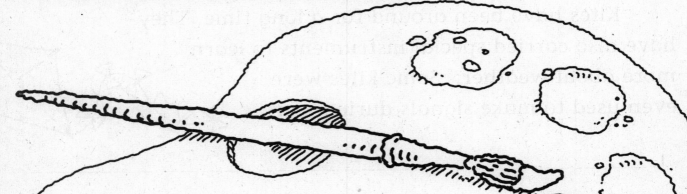

Base Word	+ -ed	+ -ing
smile	_____	_____
trace	_____	_____
trade	_____	_____
vote	_____	_____
raise	_____	_____
skate	_____	_____
slice	_____	_____
whine	_____	_____
rake	_____	_____

Name _____

Using Words

Follow the directions below.

| neighbor | below | should |

1. Circle the word that means **under**.
2. Underline the word that means **a person who lives nearby**.
3. Draw a box around the word that rhymes with **would**.

Use words from the box to complete the sentences and question below.

1. Jason lives next door to Kayla. Jason is

   Kayla's _____ .

2. Kayla lets Jason's cat sleep under her window.

   The cat sleeps _____ the window.

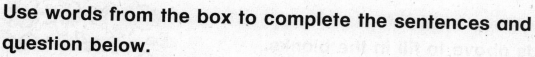

3. Kayla is a good neighbor to Jason. What

   _____ Jason be to Kayla?

Name _____

Match Up

Draw a line from each word to its meaning.

1. event   a good feeling about oneself

2. mural   a huge wall painting

3. pride   a picture of a view

4. project   a job that takes several days to do

5. scene   quickly made drawings

6. sketches   something that happens

Use the words above to fill in the blanks.

The science fair is a big _____. This

year Evelyn worked on a special _____. She

made a volcano. First, she made some _____

to show how the volcano would look.

That day, she spoke with _____ when

she told the judges about her volcano. Next month Evelyn

is going to do a project for the art fair. She is going to

paint a _____ of a snow _____.

Name _____

Solving Problems Chart

As you read the story, fill in the problems and ideas you read about. Write the solution to each problem.

Solving Problems Chart

Problems	Ideas	Solution
The class must make a _____ for the open house.	**Page 376:** 1. Print a banner. 2. _____ 3. _____ 4. _____	_____ _____ _____ _____
The class needs help to paint the _____.	**Page 393:** 1. _____ _____ 2. _____ _____ 3. _____ _____	_____ _____ _____ _____

Name _____

Story Sense

Write *True* or *Not True* after each sentence.

1. Mei Lee's idea was to paint a mural. _____

2. Mei Lee got her idea from a picture in a book.

   _____

3. The class decided which idea to use by picking

   a slip from a basket. _____

4. Twenty-five people voted for the mural.

   _____

5. All the children in Mei Lee's class worked on

   the mural. _____

6. Parents were not allowed to help the children

   work on the mural. _____

7. Children, parents, and other visitors came to

   the open house. _____

8. The people cheered when Mr. Ford told about

   the mural. _____

Name _____

Problem Solving

Read this story. Complete the chart on page 200.

Working It Out

Lane and Frank were working on a school project. When they began the project, they had some problems. Lane wanted to build a castle. Frank wanted to build a fort. Lane had an idea. She wrote "castle" and "fort" on two strips of paper. She folded the strips and put them in a box. Frank picked the strip that said "castle."

Next the children drew sketches of the castle. Frank's sketch was very different from Lane's. Frank sketched a new picture that used both of their ideas. Lane liked the new plan.

Then the children talked about what to use to make the castle. Frank suggested cardboard. He wanted to glue sand onto the cardboard to make the castle look like stone. But the sand would not stick. Lane said they should use sandpaper instead. The sandpaper worked much better.

The castle was finally done, but it tilted to one side. Frank thought he knew how to fix it. He got a piece of wood. Lane helped him prop up the castle with the wood.

Name _____

Problem Solving continued

**Tell what kinds of problems and solutions
are described in the story.**

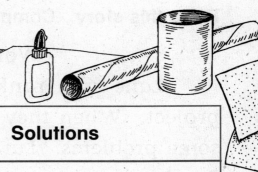

Problems	Solutions

Long *i*

Use words from the box to complete this letter from one friend to another.

Dear Ashley,

Last _____ my cousins

came to visit. We had so much fun. First we

_____ to scare each other with

scary stories. My little sister was so scared

she almost _____. Then we had

a pillow _____. When my mother

saw the mess in the living room, she just gave a

big _____. My cousins

_____ come back next month.

I hope you can come and visit me.

                              Your friend,
                              Terry

Word Bank

cried

fight

dried

might

night

sigh

tight

tried

Write a reply on a separate sheet of paper.
Use some of the words from the box.

Words with *-ed* or *-ing*

Each Spelling Word is made up of a base
word and the ending **-ed** or **-ing**. The base
word has the vowel-consonant-**e** pattern.
The final **e** in the base word is dropped
before **-ed** or **-ing** is added.

► tease – e + ing ⟶ teasing
► decide – e + ed ⟶ decided

Write the Spelling Words that end with *-ed.*

chased

_____

_____

_____

Write the Spelling Words that end with *-ing.*

hiding

_____

_____

_____

Spelling Words

1. liked
2. hoping
3. baked
4. using
5. chased
6. making
7. closed
8. hiding
9. named
10. riding

202   Theme 6: **Talent Show**

Name _____

Spelling Spree

**Unscramble the letters to make a spelling word
that completes each sentence.**

Spelling Words

1. liked
2. hoping
3. baked
4. using
5. chased
6. making
7. closed
8. hiding
9. named
10. riding

1. l d s e o c

Nicholas ___ ___ ___ ___ ___ ___
the door behind him.

2. p n g h o i

Jacob is ___ ___ ___ ___ ___ ___
to get a bike for his birthday.

3. e b k d a

Don and his dad ___ ___ ___ ___ ___
a cake.

4. n u s g i

Is Jesse ___ ___ ___ ___ ___ the right
tool for the job?

5. d a n m e

Sara ___ ___ ___ ___ ___ her dog Cowboy.

6. d i i g h n

Minh is ___ ___ ___ ___ ___ ___ behind the couch.

Name _____

Proofreading and Writing

Proofreading Irene wrote a postcard to her
uncle about a trip to the zoo. Circle four
misspelled Spelling Words in the postcard.
Write each word correctly.

Spelling Words

1. liked
2. hoping
3. baked
4. using
5. chased
6. making
7. closed
8. hiding
9. named
10. riding

Dear Uncle Howard,

   I likd going to the zoo. It was fun. We
saw all kinds of animals. We saw a baby kangaroo
ridding in its mother's pouch. We also saw two lion
cubs. They were so cute when they chaseed each
other. Billy was makeing faces at the monkeys, but
they didn't seem to mind. The monkeys were using
their tails to hang from trees.

                              Your friend,

                              Terry

1. _____   3. _____

2. _____   4. _____

✏ **Write a Postcard** On a separate piece of paper, write a
postcard to a friend or family member describing a trip.
Use Spelling Words from the list.

Name _____

Picking Meanings

Read the words and their meanings. Decide which meaning fits each sentence. Write the correct meaning.

band	past	pick
1. a musical group	1. to go beside	1. to choose
2. a stripe	2. the time in which something has already happened	2. to pull off or gather one by one

1. Mandy painted a **band** of green across the top of the mural. _____

2. The school **band** played at the football game.

   _____

3. Omar walked **past** the water fountain on his way to class. _____

4. The story takes place 100 years in the **past**.

   _____

5. The children like to **pick** apples off the tree.

   _____

6. Connor didn't know which toy to **pick**.

   _____

Name _____

Large, Larger, Largest

Add **-er** to adjectives to compare two people or things.
Add **-est** to adjectives to compare more than two people or things.

Draw pictures to show the difference among the adjectives.

Example:		
large	larger	largest

1. small	smaller	smallest

2. big	bigger	biggest

3. tall	taller	tallest

Name _____

Endings That Compare

Write a word from the box to complete each sentence.

Word Bank

| tallest | thinner | slowest | sillier | closest |

1. The horse looks _____
   than the clown.

2. The toy car is _____
   to the box.

3. Julie is the _____
   child.

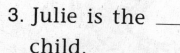

4. The snake is _____
   than the fat lizard.

5. The turtle is the _____
   animal in the race.

Name _____

Bouncing Adjectives

**Read the story about a basketball game. Circle four
adjectives that are not used correctly. Write them
correctly.**

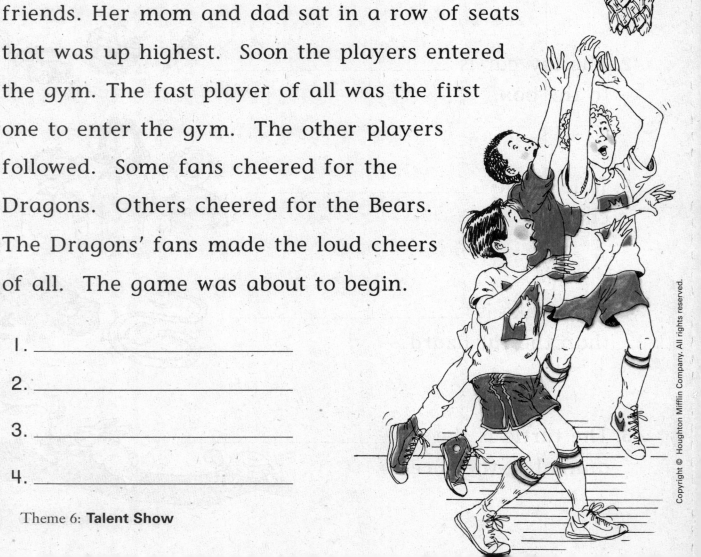

     Sandy and her parents wanted to see
Sandy's brother Randall play in the basketball
game. The crowd at the gym was biggest
than the crowd last week. Sandy sat with her
friends. Her mom and dad sat in a row of seats
that was up highest. Soon the players entered
the gym. The fast player of all was the first
one to enter the gym. The other players
followed. Some fans cheered for the
Dragons. Others cheered for the Bears.
The Dragons' fans made the loud cheers
of all. The game was about to begin.

1. _____

2. _____

3. _____

4. _____

Name _____

Alike or Different?

**Think of two stories you have read. Use the chart to tell
how the stories are different and how they are the same.**

Different	Same	Different
Title of Story 1:		Title of Story 2:

Story Comparisons

Cassie and Juan have each read a folktale. Both stories are about a rabbit that is in a race with a turtle. In Cassie's story, the two animals decide to have some fun by racing each other. In Juan's story, the two animals decide to have a race to show who is better. At the end of Cassie's folktale, the rabbit wins the race. At the end of Juan's folktale, the turtle tricks the rabbit and wins the race.

Write what is similar and what is different about the stories that Cassie and Juan read.

Cassie's Story	Both	Juan's Story
_____	_____	_____
_____	_____	_____
_____	_____	_____
_____	_____	_____
_____	_____	_____
_____	_____	_____

Name _____

Writing a Personal Narrative

Use what you have learned about taking tests to help you write about something that has happened to you. Take some time to plan what you will write. This practice will help you when you take this kind of test.

In *The School Mural*, the children plan and paint a mural to celebrate the school's fiftieth birthday. Write about a time when you took part in a big event at school or outside of school. What was the event? What did you do? How did you feel?

_____

_____

_____

_____

_____

_____

_____

Name _____

Writing a Personal Narrative

continued

Read your personal narrative. Check to be sure that

► the beginning makes your reader want to keep reading
► the narrative sticks to the topic
► there are details that tell what, who, why, when, and where
► the last part tells how you felt
► there are few mistakes in capitalization, punctuation, grammar, or spelling

Now pick one way to make your personal narrative better.

Make your changes below.

_____

_____

_____

_____

_____

_____

Name _____

Spelling Review

Write Spelling Words from the list to answer the questions.

1–6. Which words have a vowel sound spelled oo?

1. _____   4. _____

2. _____   5. _____

3. _____   6. _____

7–15. Which words have the long i sound?

7. _____   12. _____

8. _____   13. _____

9. _____   14. _____

10. _____   15. _____

11. _____

16–22. Which words end with ed or ing?

16. _____   20. _____

17. _____   21. _____

18. _____   22. _____

19. _____

Spelling Words

1. named
2. high
3. zoo
4. moon
5. liked
6. good
7. night
8. mind
9. riding
10. took
11. sky
12. using
13. hoping
14. room
15. find
16. making
17. hook
18. light
19. chased
20. fly

Name _____

Spelling Spree

Short Cuts **Add letters to each word to make a Spelling Word. Write it on the line.**

1. din _____

2. has _____

3. to _____

4. sing _____

5. go _____

Spelling Words

1. room
2. good
3. liked
4. took
5. riding
6. night
7. chased
8. light
9. hook
10. using

Rhyme Time **Finish the sentences. Write the Spelling Word that rhymes with the word in dark print. Be sure each sentence makes sense!**

6. The campers **hiked** as often as they _____ .

7. Did you see the **book** beside that _____ ?

8. It is never **bright** in the dark of _____ .

9. I saw a mouse **zoom** across the _____ .

10. Do you think you **might** turn on the _____ ?

Proofreading and Writing

Proofreading Circle four Spelling Words that are wrong in this talent show review. Then write each word correctly.

At the talent show, one girl walked on hihg stilts. One boy's bird could fli with a flag in its beak! Another child could finde any city on a map. Two children were nameed the top winners.

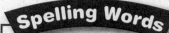

Spelling Words

1. named
2. moon
3. high
4. making
5. mind
6. fly
7. find
8. hoping
9. zoo
10. sky

1. _____   3. _____

2. _____   4. _____

Missing Letters Write the missing letters in the Spelling Words below.

5. m __ __ n   8. z __ __

6. s __ y   9. m __ __ ing

7. hop __ __ __   10. m __ __ d

Write a Description On another sheet of paper, write about a talent show act. Use Spelling Review Words.

My Handbook

Contents

Trace and write the letters.

Aa Aa

Bb Bb

Cc Cc

Dd Dd

Ee Ee

Ff Ff

Gg Gg

Trace and write the letters.

Hh Hh

Ii Ii

Jj Jj

Kk Kk

Ll Ll

Mm Mm

Trace and write the letters.

Nn Nn

Oo Oo

Pp Pp

Qq Qq

Rr Rr

Ss Ss

Tt Tt

Trace and write the letters.

Uu Uu

Vv Vv

Ww Ww

Xx Xx

Yy Yy

Zz Zz

Trace and write the letters.

Aa Aa

Bb Bb

Cc Cc

Dd Dd

Ee Ee

Ff Ff

Gg Gg

Trace and write the letters.

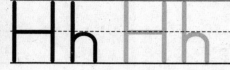 Hh Hh

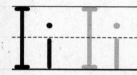 Ii Ii

Jj Jj

Kk Kk

Ll Ll

Mm Mm

Trace and write the letters.

N n N n

O o O o

P p P p

Q q Q q

R r R r

S s S s

T t T t

Trace and write the letters.

Uu Uu

Vv Vv

Ww Ww

Xx Xx

Yy Yy

Zz Zz

How to Study a Word

1. LOOK at the word.
- ► What does the word mean?
- ► What letters are in the word?
- ► Name and touch each letter.

2. SAY the word.
- ► Listen for the consonant sounds.
- ► Listen for the vowel sounds.

3. THINK about the word.
- ► How is each sound spelled?
- ► Close your eyes and picture the word.
- ► What other words have the same spelling patterns?

4. WRITE the word.
- ► Think about the sounds and the letters.
- ► Form the letters correctly.

5. CHECK the spelling.
- ► Did you spell the word the same way it is spelled in your word list?
- ► Write the word again if you did not spell it correctly.

A
about
again
a lot
always
am
and
any
are
around
as

B
back
because
been
before

C
cannot
caught
come
coming
could

D
do
does
done
down

E
enough

F
family
first
for
found
friend
from

G
getting
girl
goes
going

H
has
have
heard
her
here
his
how

I
I'd
if
I'll
I'm
into

it
it's

K
knew
know

L
letter
little

M
many
more
my
myself

N
name
never
new
now

O
of
off
on
once
one
other
our
outside

P
people
pretty

R
really
right

S
said
school
some
something
started
stopped

T
that's
the
their
there
they
thought
through
time
to
today
too

tried
two

V
very

W
want
was
went
were
what
when
where
who
will
would
write

Y
you
your

Amazing Animals:
Reading-Writing Workshop

Look carefully at how these words are spelled.

Spelling Words

1. done	7. I'll
2. one	8. around
3. two	9. found
4. back	10. once
5. some	11. girl
6. your	12. into

Challenge Words

1. knew
2. pretty

My Study List
Add your own spelling words on the back. ➡

229

Officer Buckle and Gloria

The Vowel + _r_ Sound in _car_

vowel + **r** sound ➡ c**ar**, sm**ar**t

Spelling Words

1. car	7. barn
2. smart	8. hard
3. arm	9. party
4. park	10. farm
5. yard	11. are
6. part	12. warm

Challenge Words

1. department
2. carpet

My Study List
Add your own spelling words on the back. ➡

229

Take-Home Word List

Name_____

 My Study List

1. _____
2. _____
3. _____
4. _____
5. _____
6. _____
7. _____
8. _____
9. _____
10. _____

Review Words

1. start
2. far

How to Study a Word

Look at the word.
Say the word.
Think about the word.
Write the word.
Check the spelling.

Take-Home Word List

Name_____

 My Study List

1. _____
2. _____
3. _____
4. _____
5. _____
6. _____
7. _____
8. _____
9. _____
10. _____

How to Study a Word

Look at the word.
Say the word.
Think about the word.
Write the word.
Check the spelling.

The Great Ball Game

More Long *o* Spellings

long **o** sound → g**o**ld

b**oa**t

sl**ow**

Spelling Words

1. boat
2. cold
3. road
4. blow
5. gold
6. old
7. load
8. snow
9. hold
10. most
11. toe
12. do

Challenge Words

1. goal
2. rainbow

Ant

Words That End with *nd*, *ng*, or *nk*

nd → ha**nd**

ng → ki**ng**

nk → tha**nk**

Spelling Words

1. king
2. thank
3. hand
4. sing
5. send
6. think
7. bring
8. bang
9. end
10. thing

Challenge Words

1. grand
2. young

My Study List
Add your own spelling words on the back. →

My Study List
Add your own spelling words on the back. →

Take-Home Word List

 My Study List

1. _____
2. _____
3. _____
4. _____
5. _____
6. _____
7. _____
8. _____
9. _____
10. _____

Review Words

1. and
2. long

How to Study a Word

Look at the word.
Say the word.
Think about the word.
Write the word.
Check the spelling.

Take-Home Word List

 My Study List

1. _____
2. _____
3. _____
4. _____
5. _____
6. _____
7. _____
8. _____
9. _____
10. _____

Review Words

1. so
2. show

How to Study a Word

Look at the word.
Say the word.
Think about the word.
Write the word.
Check the spelling.

232

Brothers and Sisters

Words That End with *er*

the vowel + **r** sound → flow**er**

wat**er**

Spelling Words

1. flower
2. water
3. under
4. over
5. better
6. sister
7. brother
8. mother
9. father
10. after

Challenge Words

1. other
2. center

My Study List
Add your own spelling words on the back. ➡

Amazing Animals: Spelling Review

Spelling Words

1. farm
2. bring
3. hold
4. park
5. thing
6. boat
7. smart
8. sing
9. snow
10. yard
11. thank
12. blow
13. load
14. party
15. hand
16. most
17. cold
18. think
19. send
20. road

Challenge Words

1. department
2. grand
3. young
4. goal
5. rainbow

My Study List
Add your own spelling words on the back. ➡

Take-Home Word List

Name_____

 My Study List

1. _____
2. _____
3. _____
4. _____
5. _____
6. _____
7. _____
8. _____
9. _____
10. _____

How to Study a Word

Look at the word.
Say the word.
Think about the word.
Write the word.
Check the spelling.

234

Take-Home Word List

Name_____

 My Study List

1. _____
2. _____
3. _____
4. _____
5. _____
6. _____
7. _____
8. _____
9. _____
10. _____

Review Words

1. that
2. shop

How to Study a Word

Look at the word.
Say the word.
Think about the word.
Write the word.
Check the spelling.

234

Take-Home Word List

Jalapeño Bagels

Contractions

A contraction is a short way of writing one or more words. An apostrophe replaces any dropped letters.

Spelling Words

1. I'll
2. we've
3. I'm
4. you're
5. isn't
6. didn't
7. you'll
8. I've
9. it's
10. we'll
11. can't

Challenge Words

1. they're
2. wouldn't

Family Time:
Reading-Writing Workshop
Look carefully at how these words are spelled.

Spelling Words

1. who
2. a lot
3. were
4. many
5. our
6. friend
7. cannot
8. here
9. first
10. today
11. would
12. could

Challenge Words

1. heard
2. again

My Study List
Add your own spelling words on the back. ➜

My Study List
Add your own spelling words on the back. ➜

Take-Home Word List

Name_____

 My Study List

1. _____
2. _____
3. _____
4. _____
5. _____
6. _____
7. _____
8. _____
9. _____
10. _____

How to Study a Word

Look at the word.
Say the word.
Think about the word.
Write the word.
Check the spelling.

Take-Home Word List

Name_____

 My Study List

1. _____
2. _____
3. _____
4. _____
5. _____
6. _____
7. _____
8. _____
9. _____
10. _____

Review Words

1. it
2. us

How to Study a Word

Look at the word.
Say the word.
Think about the word.
Write the word.
Check the spelling.

Thunder Cake

Words That End with *-ed* or *-ing*

bat + t + ed ➝ ba**tted**

run + n + ing ➝ ru**nning**

Spelling Words

1. batted
2. running
3. clapped
4. stopped
5. getting
6. shopping
7. stepped
8. hugging
9. pinned
10. sitting

Challenge Words

1. jogging
2. flipped

My Study List
Add your own spelling words on the back. ➝

Carousel

The Final Sound in *puppy*

puppy ➝ pup p**y**

baby ➝ ba b**y**

Spelling Words

1. puppy
2. baby
3. lucky
4. happy
5. very
6. lady
7. funny
8. silly
9. many
10. only
11. cookie

Challenge Words

1. furry
2. angry

My Study List
Add your own spelling words on the back. ➝

Take-Home Word List

Name_____

 My Study List

1. _____
2. _____
3. _____
4. _____
5. _____
6. _____
7. _____
8. _____
9. _____
10. _____

Review Words

1. me
2. bee

How to Study a Word

Look at the word.
Say the word.
Think about the word.
Write the word.
Check the spelling.

Take-Home Word List

Name_____

 My Study List

1. _____
2. _____
3. _____
4. _____
5. _____
6. _____
7. _____
8. _____
9. _____
10. _____

Review Words

1. this
2. must

How to Study a Word

Look at the word.
Say the word.
Think about the word.
Write the word.
Check the spelling.

The Art Lesson

The Vowel Sounds in *moon* and *book*

moon ➔ z**oo**, f**oo**d

book ➔ h**oo**k, t**oo**k

Spelling Words

1. zoo
2. tooth
3. hook
4. moon
5. book
6. soon
7. took
8. good
9. room
10. foot
11. you
12. who

Challenge Words

1. hoof
2. school

My Study List
Add your own
spelling words
on the back. ➔

Family Time: Spelling Review

Spelling Words

1. better
2. isn't
3. happy
4. clapped
5. sister
6. I'll
7. lady
8. stopped
9. sitting
10. brother
11. I'm
12. baby
13. getting
14. mother
15. you're
16. puppy
17. hugging
18. I've
19. silly
20. it's

Challenge Words

1. other
2. they're
3. wouldn't
4. angry
5. jogging

My Study List
Add your own
spelling words
on the back. ➔

Name_____

 My Study List

1. _____

2. _____

3. _____

4. _____

5. _____

6. _____

7. _____

8. _____

9. _____

10. _____

How to Study a Word

Look at the word.
Say the word.
Think about the word.
Write the word.
Check the spelling.

Name_____

 My Study List

1. _____

2. _____

3. _____

4. _____

5. _____

6. _____

7. _____

8. _____

9. _____

10. _____

Review Words

1. too
2. cook

How to Study a Word

Look at the word.
Say the word.
Think about the word.
Write the word.
Check the spelling.

Moses Goes to a Concert

More Long *i* Spellings

the long **i** sound → sky

find

n**igh**t

Spelling Words

1. sky	7. light
2. find	8. dry
3. night	9. right
4. high	10. mind
5. fly	11. eye
6. try	12. buy

Challenge Words

1. flight
2. reply

My Study List
Add your own
spelling words
on the back. →

Talent Show:
Reading-Writing Workshop

Look carefully at how these words are spelled.

Spelling Words

1. tried	7. other
2. never	8. started
3. going	9. something
4. coming	10. school
5. new	11. outside
6. very	12. people

Challenge Words

1. enough
2. through

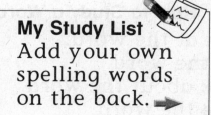

My Study List
Add your own
spelling words
on the back. →

Take-Home Word List

Name_____

 My Study List

1. _____
2. _____
3. _____
4. _____
5. _____
6. _____
7. _____
8. _____
9. _____
10. _____

How to Study a Word
Look at the word.
Say the word.
Think about the word.
Write the word.
Check the spelling.

242

Take-Home Word List

Name_____

 My Study List

1. _____
2. _____
3. _____
4. _____
5. _____
6. _____
7. _____
8. _____
9. _____
10. _____

Review Words
1. why
2. my

How to Study a Word
Look at the word.
Say the word.
Think about the word.
Write the word.
Check the spelling.

242

Talent Show:
Spelling Review

Spelling Words

1. took	11. hook
2. fly	12. mind
3. good	13. using
4. riding	14. liked
5. high	15. making
6. room	16. zoo
7. night	17. light
8. find	18. named
9. chased	19. sky
10. hoping	20. moon

Challenge Words

1. school
2. reply
3. flight
4. teasing
5. decided

My Study List
Add your own spelling words on the back. ➡

The School Mural

More Words with -ed or -ing

like − e + ed ➡ lik**ed**

hope − e + ing ➡ hop**ing**

Spelling Words

1. liked	6. making
2. hoping	7. closed
3. baked	8. hiding
4. using	9. named
5. chased	10. riding

Challenge Words

1. teasing
2. decided

My Study List
Add your own spelling words on the back. ➡

Take-Home Word List

Take-Home Word List

Name_____

 My Study List

1. _____
2. _____
3. _____
4. _____
5. _____
6. _____
7. _____
8. _____
9. _____
10. _____

Review Words

1. time
2. sleep

How to Study a Word

Look at the word.
Say the word.
Think about the word.
Write the word.
Check the spelling.

Name_____

 My Study List

1. _____
2. _____
3. _____
4. _____
5. _____
6. _____
7. _____
8. _____
9. _____
10. _____

How to Study a Word

Look at the word.
Say the word.
Think about the word.
Write the word.
Check the spelling.

Read each question. Check your paper for each kind of mistake. Correct any mistakes you find.

☐ Did I begin each sentence with a capital letter?

☐ Did I use the correct end mark?

☐ Did I spell each word correctly?

☐ Did I indent each paragraph?

Proofreading Marks

∧	Add one or more words.	I see the play. *(want to added above ∧)*
——	Take out one or more words. Change the spelling.	The boat ~~did~~ moved slowly. The cloud ~~filed~~ the sky. *(filled)*
/	Make a capital letter a small letter.	The A̸nimals hid from the storm.
≡	Make a small letter a capital letter.	There are thirty days in a̲p̲ril.

A	A	A	B	B	C	C	D	D
E	E	E	F	F	G	G	H	H
I	I	J	J	K	K	L	L	M
M	N	N	O	O	P	P	Q	Q
R	R	S	S	T	T	U	U	V
V	W	W	X	X	Y	Y	Z	Z

You can add punctuation marks or other letters to the blanks.

Letter Tray
↓

Letter Tray

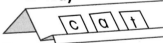
c a t

fold

d	d	c	c	b	b	a	a	a
h	h	g	g	f	f	e	e	e
m	l	l	k	k	j	j	i	i
q	q	p	p	o	o	n	n	m
v	u	u	t	t	s	s	r	r
z	z	y	y	x	x	w	w	v

Jalapeño Bagels	The Great Ball Game	Officer Buckle and Gloria
early	ago	board
hair	field	listen
instead	half	told
Carousel	Brothers & Sisters	Ant
aunt	middle	between
million	trouble	care
pair	uncle	weigh

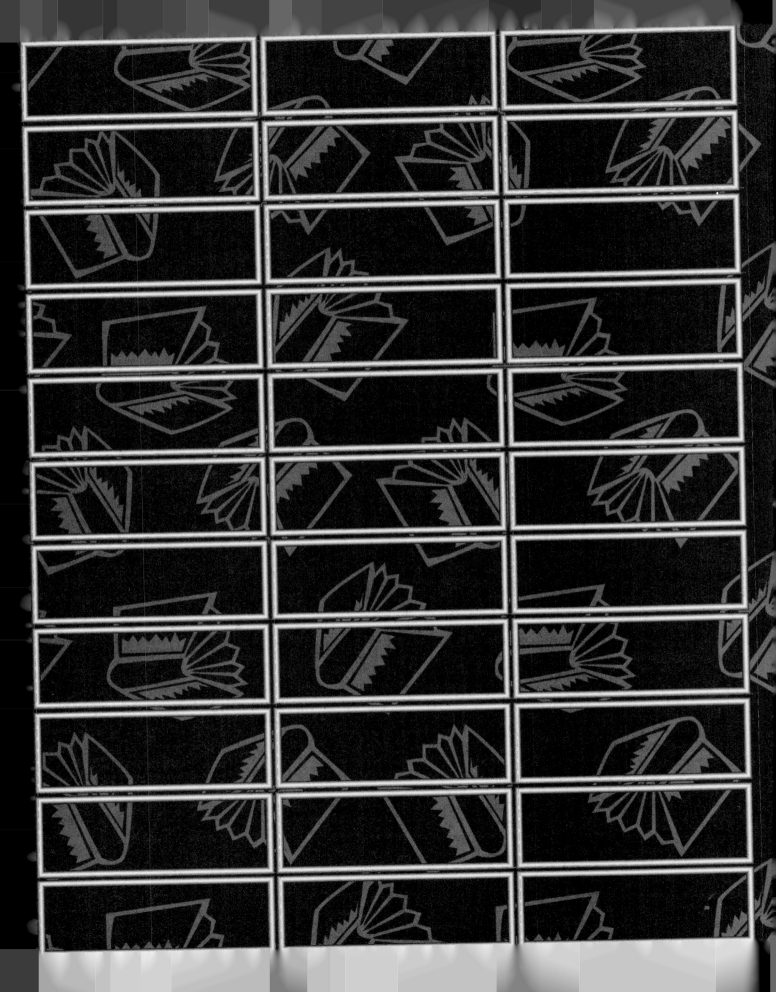

	Moses Goes to a Concert	Thunder Cake
	alphabet	air
	heart	child
	mind	heavy
	The School Mural	hour
	below	The Art Lesson
	neighbor	fair
	should	gold
		woman

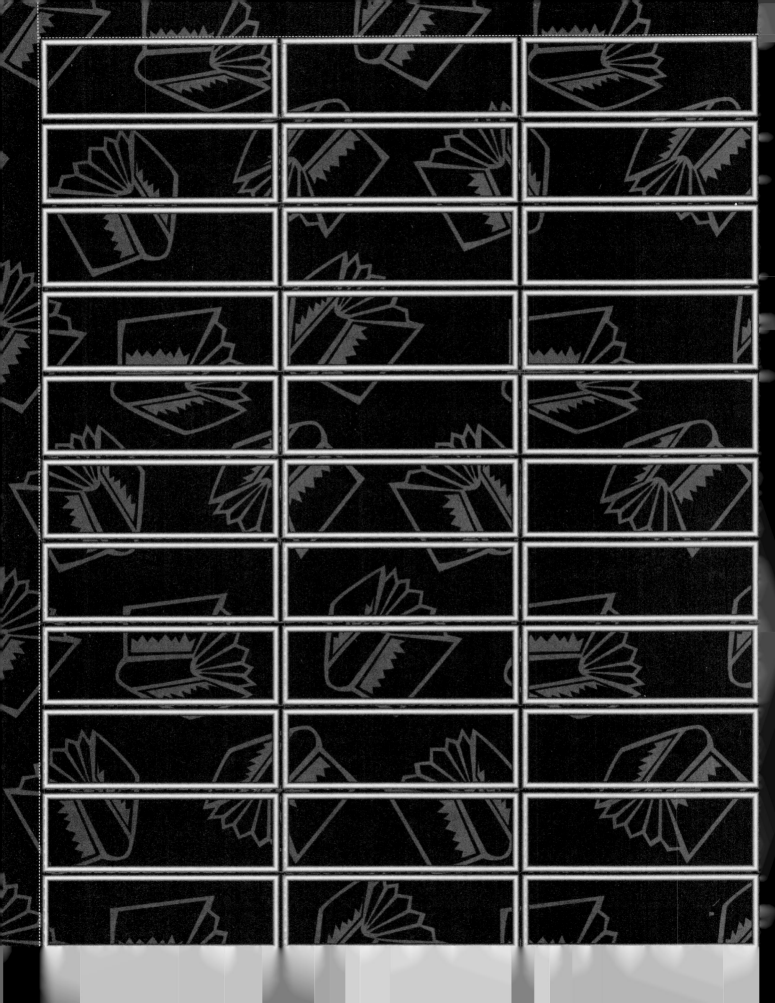